ASSESSING ENGLISH LANGUAGE LEARNERS

Assessing English Language Learners explains and illustrates the main ideas underlying assessment as an activity intimately linked to instruction and the basic principles for developing, using, selecting, and adapting assessment instruments and strategies to assess content knowledge in English language learners (ELLs). Sensitive to the professional development needs of both in-service and pre-service mainstream teachers with ELLs in their classrooms and those receiving formal training to teach culturally and linguistically diverse students, the text is designed to engage readers in:

- viewing assessment as a critical part of teaching
- appreciating that assessments provide teachers with valuable information about their students' learning and thinking
- becoming aware of the relationship among language, culture, and testing
- understanding the reasoning that guides test construction
- recognizing the limitations of testing practices
- being confident that assessment is an activity classroom teachers (not only accountability specialists) can perform.

Highlighting alternative, multidisciplinary approaches that address linguistic and cultural diversity in testing, this text, enhanced by multiple field-tested exercises and examples of different forms of assessment, is ideal for any course covering the theory and practice of ELL assessment.

Guillermo Solano-Flores is Professor of Education at the Graduate School of Education, Stanford University, USA.

ASSESSING ENGLISH LANGUAGE LEARNERS

Theory and Practice

Guillermo Solano-Flores

Routledge
Taylor & Francis Group

NEW YORK AND LONDON

First published 2016
by Routledge
711 Third Avenue, New York, NY 10017

and by Routledge
2 Park Square, Milton Park, Abingdon, Oxon, OX14 4RN

Routledge is an imprint of the Taylor & Francis Group, an informa business

© 2016 Taylor & Francis

The right of Guillermo Solano-Flores to be identified as author of this work has been asserted by him in accordance with sections 77 and 78 of the Copyright, Designs and Patents Act 1988.

Library of Congress Cataloging in Publication Data
Solano-Flores, Guillermo, 1955-
Assessing English language learners : theory and practice / by Guillermo Solano-Flores.
pages cm
Includes bibliographical references.
ISBN 978-0-415-81928-2 (hardback)
ISBN 978-0-415-81929-9 (pbk.)
ISBN 978-0-203-52195-3 (ebook)
1. English language—Study and teaching—United States—Evaluation.
2. Educational tests and measurements—United States. I. Title.
PE1128.A2S5946 2016
428.0076—dc23
2015027197

ISBN: 978-0-415-81928-2 (hbk)
ISBN: 978-0-415-81929-9 (pbk)
ISBN: 978-0-203-52195-3 (ebk)

Typeset in Bembo
by diacriTech, Chennai

BRIEF CONTENTS

CONTENTS

INTRODUCTION

This book is intended to support educators to meet the challenges of effectively teaching and assessing students in linguistically diverse classrooms in an era of accountability, large-scale assessment, and the Common Core State Standards. To meet these challenges, educators need to be able to perform assessment activities and interpret assessment information in ways that allow them to make sound instructional decisions in support of students who are English language learners.

While the term *English language learners* (ELLs) is widely used in the field of education in the US, it is not explicit about the fact that these students are developing two languages. The book embraces the view of ELL students as emergent bilinguals—individuals who already have a language and are, in addition, developing a second language through their experiences at school (García, Kleifgen, & Falchi, 2008). This view allows appreciation of the richness of these students' linguistic resources and is consistent with current knowledge in the fields of second language acquisition and sociolinguistics. Moreover, this view is critical to ensuring valid, meaningful assessment practices for ELL students (see Valdés, Menken, & Castro, 2015).

Frequent, mandatory testing for all students with accountability purposes is an increasingly powerful force that drives today's schools' activities. Yet there is considerable room for teachers to benefit from programs that support them to improve their assessment practices (Borko, Mayfield, Marion, Flexer, & Cumbo, 1997; Martínez, Stecher, & Borko, 2009).

When cultural and linguistic diversity are considered, it becomes evident that the needs for enhanced assessment skills among teachers are even more serious. Policy concerning schooling and testing for ELLs is not necessarily based on current knowledge from the language sciences (Hakuta, 2000) or its interpretation and implementation is inconsistent (Menken & García, 2010). Also, there is a chronic shortage of teachers with formal training in the teaching of culturally and linguistically diverse students (Darling-Hammond & Skyes, 2003; Sleeter, 2001). Moreover, existing programs on cultural and linguistic diversity may face serious challenges promoting higher-order thinking skills regarding assessment practices for ELL students among teachers who teach these students (Nguyen-Le, 2010).

The content of this book is based on four premises:

First Premise: *In order to properly serve their students, educators need to appropriate assessment as part of their teaching practices.* Effective support for ELL students cannot happen without collaborative work through which teachers develop strategies that are sensitive to the linguistic diversity of their schools (Johnson & Freeman, 2010). Educators need to be actors, rather than observers, in the assessment process (Solano-Flores & Soltero-González, 2011). Thus, the book promotes the ability to develop, review, and adapt assessment activities and instruments. Assessment development is viewed as a valuable professional development activity that helps teachers to both obtain high quality information about their ELL students' progress towards learning goals and improve their teaching skills.

Second Premise: *In order for that process of cultural appropriation to take place, educators need to appreciate how concepts and ideas typically used in the context of large-scale assessment are also relevant to their practice.* Especially important is the notion of sampling. According to a sampling perspective, assessment instruments and activities can be viewed as samples of observations. The inclusion of ELL students in classroom assessment activities is critical for teachers to make sound instructional decisions.

Third Premise: *In order to use assessment effectively, teachers need to view assessment as a multidisciplinary endeavor.* As with many books on assessment, this book introduces the reader to the reasoning and main concepts of psychometrics—the discipline concerned with measuring behavior, knowledge, and skills in humans and social systems. However, unlike those other books on assessment, this book examines this reasoning and these concepts from the perspective of disciplines concerned with language, cognition, and culture. Reasoning and knowledge from the fields of language development and sociolinguistics allow proper examination of that process for ELL students. Knowledge from the field of cognitive science allows reasoning about assessment in terms of learning and thinking processes; it also allows making meaningful interpretations of the performance of ELL students on tests. Familiarity with concepts such as bilingualism, language contact, and dialect will support teachers in developing a deep understanding of language proficiency and the nature of linguistic groups. Also, understanding how culture shapes mind will help teachers to identify the characteristics of different student populations that are relevant to developing assessments and interpreting information produced by assessment activities and instruments. **Fourth Premise***: In order to make assessment work to the benefit of their ELL students, teachers need to become critical users of assessment information and creative developers of assessment instruments and assessment activities.* Teachers need to strengthen their ability to use assessment information judiciously and to create or adapt assessment instruments in ways that allow them to effectively support the learning of their ELL students. Consistent with the view that teachers are not only educators, but also evaluators, communicators, and agents of socialization (Fillmore & Snow, 2010), the book embraces an integral perspective of teaching practices. According to this perspective, fair, valid, and meaningful assessment practices need to be enacted through these multiple roles, not simply by applying certain assessment concepts and procedures. As the book shows, to be creative and to develop critical thinking skills with regard to assessment, teachers need to revise their own teaching practices and to make a deliberate effort to address the complexities of language through improved social interaction with their ELL students.

References

Borko, H., Mayfield, V., Marion, S., Flexer, R., & Cumbo, K. (1997). Teacher's developing ideas and practices about mathematics performance assessment: Successes, stumbling blocks, and implications for professional development. *Teaching and Teacher Education, 13*, 3, 259–278.

Darling-Hammond, L. & Sykes, G. (2003, September 17). Wanted: A national teacher supply policy for education: The right way to meet the "Highly Qualified Teacher" challenge. *Education Policy Analysis Archives, 11*(33). Retrieved July 31, 2015 from http://epaa.asu.edu/epaa/v11n33/.

Fillmore, L. W. & Snow, C. (2000). *What teachers need to know about language.* Washington, DC: ERIC Clearinghouse on Languages and Linguistics Special Report.

García, O., Kleifgen, A., & Falchi, L. (2008). *From English language learners to emergent bilinguals.* Equity Matters: Research Review No. 1.

Hakuta, K. (2000). *How long does it take English learners to attain proficiency?* University of California Linguistic Minority Research Institute. Policy Reports. Santa Barbara: Linguistic Minority Research Institute. Retrieved July 28, 2009 from http://repositories.cdlib.org/lmri/pr/hakuta.

Johnson, D. C. & Freeman, R. (2010). In K. Menken & O. García (Eds.), *Negotiating language policies in schools: Educators as policymakers* (pp. 13–31). New York: Routledge.

Martínez, J. F., Stecher, B., & Borko, H. (2009). Classroom assessment practices, teacher judgments, and student achievement in mathematics: Evidence from the ECLS. *Educational Assessment, 14*, 78–102.

Menken, K. & García, O. (2010) Introduction. In K. Menken and O. García (Eds.), *Negotiating language policies in schools: Educators as policymakers* (pp. 1–10). New York: Routledge.

Nguyen-Le, K. (2010). *Personal and formal backgrounds as factors which influence linguistic and cultural competency in the teaching of mathematics.* Doctoral dissertation. University of Colorado Boulder.

Sleeter, C. E. (2001). Preparing teachers for culturally diverse schools: Research and the overwhelming presence of whiteness. *Journal of Teacher Education, 52*(2), 94–106.

Solano-Flores, G. & Soltero-González, L. (2011). Meaningful assessment in linguistically diverse classrooms. In B. B. Flores, R. H. Sheets, & E. R. Clark (Eds.), *Teacher preparation for bilingual student populations: Educar para transformar* (pp. 146–163). New York: Routledge.

Valdés, G., Menken, K., & Castro, M. (Eds.) (2015). *Common Core, bilingual and English language learners: A resource for educators.* Philadelphia, PA: Caslon, Inc.

1

UNDERSTANDING ASSESSMENT

Overview

This chapter introduces the reader to concepts and ideas that are critical to understanding assessment practices, especially in relation to students who are English language learners (ELLs). While some definitions are not necessarily formal, they should allow the reader to follow the ideas discussed throughout the book. Some of the concepts discussed in this chapter are discussed in more detail in Chapter 9.

The section "Multiple Facets of Assessment" provides a comprehensive view of the concept of assessment as a process, an instrument, and a system. The section "Basic Concepts in Assessment" discusses construct, measurement error, standardization, sampling, validity, reliability, and fairness.

The word *assessment* is used to refer to the activity of integrating and evaluating information relevant to student academic achievement from different sources (see Cronbach, 1990). Also, it is used to refer to "a tool designed to observe students' behavior and produce data that can be used to draw reasonable inferences about what students know" (Pellegrino, Chudowsky, & Glaser, 2001, p. 42). The terms *assessment* and *test* are used interchangeably to refer to that tool or instrument. Also, the terms *item* and *task* are used interchangeably. However, the former is used more frequently to refer to questions that require short answers from the students and the latter is used more frequently to refer to more complex activities involving constructed responses.

Multiple Facets of Assessment

Assessment as a Process

Assessment can be viewed as a process of gathering different kinds information about student achievement which, ideally, should provide "critical information for many parts of the education system, including instructional decisions, holding schools accountable for meeting learning goals, and monitoring program effectiveness" (Wilson & Bertenthal, 2006, p. 3). Assessment comprises actions taken with the intent to determine students' knowledge or skills according to a set of goals or expectations. It encompasses the reasoning and procedures used to generate tasks, score student responses, and transform the information on those responses into measures of academic achievement.

In *Knowing What Students Know*, Pellegrino, Chudowsky, and Glaser (2001) offer a simple but compelling view of assessment in terms of three components: cognition, observation, and interpretation. *Cognition* refers to the mental processes and activities underlying proficiency in a given knowledge domain. A good test should not be developed without having a clear idea of the cognitive processes involved in responding to it. As an example, take subtraction. To develop a test on this domain, we need to formalize our beliefs about the processes that take place when students solve different kinds of subtraction problems. Among many others, these processes may include retrieving information from memory, applying computation routines, and representing subtraction problems in multiple formats. Depending on how subtraction is defined, the processes may also include recognizing when a problem is a subtraction problem, and constructing strategies to solve problems through subtraction, among many other activities.

Observation refers to the kinds of tasks that elicit from students responses that show competence in the knowledge domain assessed. In the example of subtraction, depending on the knowledge and skills of interest, a test might include, among others, straight computation problems, word problems, and problems that contain complex contextual information. These problems need to be presented in different response formats, from those that involve information recognition and recall to those that involve open, elaborate responses.

Interpretation refers to the different patterns of student responses that correspond to varying levels of student competence. A test would be useless without a set of rules for determining degrees of correctness of the possible student responses. In the simplest case, we want to know which option is the correct response for each of the items in a multiple-choice test. For constructed-response tasks, there should be a set of rules that allow scorers to make decisions about the quality of the process involved in the student's response (i.e. the assumed cognitive activity that takes place during problem solving) and the product of that response (i.e. the outcome of that cognitive activity).

The process of assessment can be examined according to the contexts in which assessment takes place, the functions assessment serves, and the uses of assessments (Figure 1.1). Two assessment contexts are identified, classroom and large-scale.

Classroom assessment comprises the formal and informal assessment activities that take place in the classroom (e.g. quizzes, classroom conversations, assignments) developed, used, or selected by the teacher according to the teaching context, the instructional goals, and the teacher's knowledge of their students on aspects such as the students' progress, learning styles, or strengths and weaknesses. *Formative assessment* is embedded in instruction and takes place, for example, as a part of an instructional unit, lesson, or course; teachers use it to inform their teaching and to provide feedback to students (Black & Wiliam, 2009). In contrast, *summative classroom assessment* takes place at the end of that instructional unit, lesson, or course; teachers use it to grade their students and to serve reporting purposes.

Large-scale assessment comprises the formal assessment activities performed by entities external to the classroom, such as a state's department of education; it involves the testing of large populations of students. *Diagnostic assessment* is not embedded in instruction and may take place at the beginning of a school year with the purpose of determining, for example, the students' proficiency in English

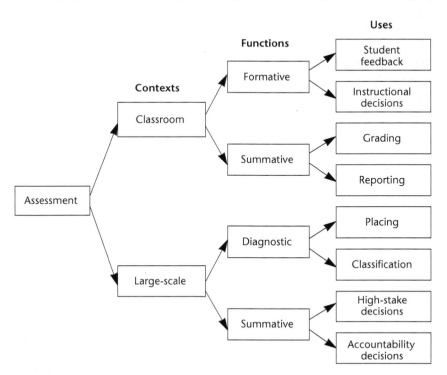

FIGURE 1.1 Contexts, functions, and uses in the assessment process.

for instructional placement decisions (e.g. bilingual, transitional, or English-only programs) or for classification decisions (e.g. to determine if it is appropriate to assume that students are proficient enough in English to be tested in that language). *Summative large-scale assessment* informs high-stake and accountability decisions such as admission, retention, or graduation for individual students.

Assessment as an Instrument

While everybody has an intuitive idea of what assessments are, a definition is needed to be able to discuss the complexities of the field of assessment:

> An *assessment* or *test* can be defined as an instrument composed by a set of tasks and their accompanying response formats, scoring systems, and administration procedures, designed to obtain information on the extent to which an individual or a population of examinees possess the knowledge or skills that are relevant to a given domain.

The term *task* is used to refer generically to any form of item, question, or problem included in a test. Tasks vary tremendously on the amount and complexity of information provided to students (e.g. directions, contextual information, data, diagrams), the knowledge and skills they are intended to address (e.g. recognizing information, evaluating, applying a procedure, solving a problem), and the kinds of activities involved in their completion (e.g. performing computations, reading a passage, writing a report, conducting experiments with various pieces of equipment).

Response format is the means by which students' responses are captured. The range of response formats is wide, from multiple-choice and fill-in-the-blank items—which restrict the variety of responses required from the student—to essays, logs, notebooks, concept maps, portfolios, and real-time observation—which lend themselves to a wide variety of responses varying in length and form.

It is well known that different types of tasks and response formats are sensitive to different aspects of knowledge. This is due to the fact that they pose different sets of cognitive demands (see Baxter, Shavelson, Goldman, & Pine, 1992; Martinez, 1999). To a large extent, this is due also to the fact that different tasks and response formants pose different sets of linguistic demands. For example, while multiple-choice items require virtually no writing and contain relatively fewer and shorter sentences than open-ended items, their grammatical structures tend to be more complex. Because of this trade-off between challenges and affordances, a simple way of addressing the challenges of validly assessing ELL students in English consists of using different types of tasks and response formats. This approach is intended to ensure that these students are exposed to different sets of linguistic challenges and affordances, thus providing them with different sets of opportunities to demonstrate their knowledge.

A *scoring system* is the set of rules based on which a score is assigned to a student's response or to one aspect of the student's response. The simplest scoring system is that of multiple-choice and certain fill-in-the-blank items in which, whether the response is correct or incorrect can be told unambiguously from the option selected or the word or short phrase written by the student. In contrast, more complex tasks and response formats (e.g. open-ended items, constructed-response tasks) involve human judgment and make it necessary the use of *scoring rubrics*—documents which describe the characteristics of student responses at various levels of correctness (see Arter & McTighe, 2000). *Holistic rubrics* focus on the overall characteristics of performance; they consist of descriptions of patterns with which student performance is observed. *Analytic rubrics* focus on the presence or absence of certain characteristics separately, regardless of how these characteristics are related.

An important challenge in the design of scoring rubrics consists of ensuring that they do not favor certain writing styles over others. This is especially important in the testing of young students from linguistic and cultural minorities. Cultures differ as to how they encourage or discourage long and short utterances among children, especially when they talk to adults (see Heath, 1983). This can be reflected in the length or degree of elaboration of written responses given by students to open-ended questions. The scoring rubrics should prevent raters from unduly valuing long responses or responses given with certain writing styles over short responses.

An *administration procedure* specifies how tasks should be given to examinees. The amount of time students are given to complete a test, whether they should complete tasks individually or in pairs, and how any materials used in the test should be distributed to students and collected from them are examples of the aspects of testing that an administration procedure should specify.

While the administration procedure is not always considered as a fundamental component of tests, its importance is more evident in the testing of ELL students and the use of *testing accommodations*—modifications on the way in which tests are administered with the purpose of minimizing the effect of ELLs' limited proficiency in the language of testing (Abedi, Hofstetter, & Lord, 2004). Providing certain testing accommodations to ELL students often requires the alteration of the administration procedure. The most obvious case is the accommodation consisting of giving these students more time to complete their tests.

Assessment as a System

The term *assessment system* refers to the coordinated work of different organizations (e.g. schools, school districts, departments of education) with the purpose of obtaining and reporting information on their students' academic achievement (see Wilson & Bertenthal, 2006). Typically, the content of instruments generated by assessment systems is aligned to normative documents such as *standards* documents. Among different types of standards documents are *content standards*, which prescribe what students should know and be able to do by grade and content area (Raizen, 1997).

State assessment systems test students of all grades every year on each of several areas such as science, mathematics, and reading. Other assessment systems test students of selected grades in cycles that are longer than a year. That is the case of the National Assessment of Educational Progress (NAEP), which tests students of Grades 4, 8, and 12 on science, reading, mathematics, and other content areas (National Center for Education Statistics, 2011).

Frequently, the public has expectations about assessment systems that do not correspond to the goals for which they were created. For example, NAEP assessments are not designed to produce full information on the competencies of individual students on a content area. Rather, they are designed to produce information about the competencies of a large population of students on a broad content area (see Mazzeo, Lazer, & Zieky, 2006).

Basic Concepts in Assessment

Construct

A central activity in the field of assessment consists of finding evidence that supports or discredits the claim that a test truly measures a given construct. *Construct* can be defined as an attribute (e.g. oral communication, understanding the laws of thermodynamics, the ability to represent a statement as a mathematical expression) that an individual may possess in varying degrees. Because it is not tangible, there is never absolute certainty that a given construct exists. However, the degree of its presence in an individual is inferred from observations such as the responses of students to items in a test (Crocker & Algina, 2008).

Test developers continuously deal with the challenge that constructs are difficult to isolate or take apart. For example, to measure the construct, *communicating ideas mathematically*, a set of tasks may be included in a mathematics test in which students are given statements such as, "Nancy took half the time John took and twice the time Mary took to finish her homework," and asked to express them as equations or number sentences, using the proper symbols and notation conventions. A statement like this poses certain reading challenges. So much so that some would argue that, because of the way in which it is written, the item assesses reading skills rather than the ability to understand and express ideas mathematically. At the same time, others would argue that understanding this kind of statement is part of the ability to understand and formalize ideas mathematically and that the content of mathematics and the language of mathematics cannot be disentangled (see Morgan, 1998; Pimm, 1987). Similar arguments could be made regarding the use of language in other disciplines (e.g. Snow, 2010).

The intricate relationship between content and language illustrates an important issue in testing—*multidimensionality,* the presence of more than one construct in a test or task. In and of itself, multidimensionality is not necessarily a problem. Rather, it is an aspect that needs to be detected and considered to decide how data on student performance need to be treated and how student test scores should be interpreted and reported (for example as test sub-scores).

Wrongly assuming *unidimensionality* in tests or items may be especially detrimental to ELL students when language factors are intimately related with the constructs a test is intended to measure. Multidimensionality, for instance, may be a source of *item bias*—a systematic item score difference that unfairly favors one population over another because the item is not actually measuring the same thing for the two populations (Camilli, 2006).

Measurement Error

Contrary to the beliefs about measurement among the general public (see Mlodinov, 2008), tests are not as precise instruments as we would like them to be. The reason is that, in a way, measuring academic achievement is more complex than measuring the physical world; test scores are influenced by multiple contextual and human factors.

The term *measurement error* refers to the extent to which measures of academic achievement are due to sources that are not the constructs a test is intended to measure. While measurement error is impossible to eliminate, it can be minimized. A great deal of what test developers and educational measurement specialists do consists of estimating measurement error and taking actions intended to minimize it (Feldt & Brennan, 1989).

Many sources of measurement error can be considered as random; they are unknown and beyond control. Such is the case of fatigue, mood, or alertness, which may affect the way in which students perform on tests but have nothing to do with the knowledge of the content being assessed. Other sources of measurement error are systematic; they are a consequence of the limitations of the measurement instruments or procedures and, to some extent, they can be controlled for. The language in which a test is administered to students can be treated as a systematic source of measurement error. By examining how the performance of a specific group of ELL students varies across languages (that is, when they are tested in English and in their first language), it is possible to determine whether it is appropriate to test a given group of ELL students in English or in its native language (Solano-Flores & Trumbull, 2008).

Standardization

Standardization is the set of actions oriented to ensuring that the characteristics of the tasks and their response formats, the conditions in which they are administered, and the procedures used to score student responses are the same for all students. Ultimately, the purpose of standardization is to ensure fair testing and to ensure, to the extent possible, that any observed score differences on a test are due to differences in the construct of interest rather than differences in the ways in which students are tested (Kane, 2006).

Advances in testing in the last decades have made it evident that standardization is a complex issue and may entail much more than ensuring constancy in the ways in which students are tested. One example of these advances comes from the field of *computer adaptive testing*, a method by which a given item posed to a student taking the test is selected based on the responses given by the student to previous items and the known levels of difficulty of those items (see Sireci & Zenisky, 2006). Another example comes from the field of international test comparisons, in which translated tests are given to students from different countries in different languages and certain adaptations are made to ensure that the contextual information they provide are culturally meaningful to all test takers (e.g. Cook & Schmitt-Cascallar, 2005). A third example comes from the field of testing accommodations, which, by definition, are modifications in the ways in which ELLs are tested (see Abedi, Hofstetter, & Lord, 2004). In these examples, different students or different groups of students may be given different sets of items or the same items but in different languages or under different conditions.

Underlying this apparent contradiction between the definition of standardization and these changes in testing practices is the tension between what is gained and what is lost when all students are tested in the same way. Administering a test in the same way to all students does not necessarily warrant fairness; also, not all modifications of the conditions in which students are tested affect the integrity of a test. Especially in assessing ELL students, deciding what testing conditions need to be kept constant across individuals or groups of students and what needs to be modified should be based on the extent to which those actions contribute significantly to minimizing measurement error.

Sampling

The notion of sampling is critical in social sciences and education because our understanding of phenomena and the decisions that we make about an object of study are necessarily based on fragmented information (see Pedhazur & Pedhazur-Schmelkin, 1991). *Sampling* is the process throughout which a portion of a whole is examined with the intent to make generalizations about the characteristics of a population or universe (the whole) based on the characteristics of the sample.

The terms *population* and *universe* do not apply only to people (as in "population of students" or "population of teachers"). Depending on the problem at hand, it is common to talk about a population of schools, states, and the like, or about a universe of observations, test items, or any category of events or cases that can be grouped. The reasons for sampling are mainly practical. Dealing with all the cases that constitute an entire population—such as a linguistic group—would be extremely costly or time-consuming.

Suppose that a study is conducted on the factors that shape the academic achievement of ELL students and that, based on the results obtained, decisions are to be made that will affect all ELL students enrolled in US public schools. Ideally, in order to be representative of the entire population of students in public schools in the US, the sample should include ELL students with different combinations of ethnicity, language background, socioeconomic status, locale (rural vs. urban), and other factors that are critical to interpreting their academic achievement scores, in the proportions in which we know they exist in the country.

The extent to which the characteristics of a sample reflect the characteristics of a population or universe determines whether it is representative of that population or universe. If a sample is representative, it is likely to lead to correct generalizations about the population or universe. If it is not representative, it is said to be a *biased sample* and is likely to lead to invalid generalizations about the population or universe.

An example used frequently to illustrate bias in sampling is the bias that results from assuming English proficiency status (i.e. being or not being an ELL) based on the students' ethnicity or last name. Whereas being an ELL is associated with being of certain ethnicity or having a last name of certain origin, not all students who belong to a given ethnic group or have certain last names are ELLs. This proxy criterion is flawed and is likely to produce many false positive and false negative classification cases—respectively, students wrongly deemed ELLs and non-ELLs.

Biased samples are undesirable because they lead to wrong conclusions. Ensuring unbiased samples is not easy in the field of education due to the complexity of social and demographic factors. For instance, should we assume that a sample is representative of the different ethnicities that exist in the US just because it includes students from the major racial groups (African American, Asian, Latino, and White)? Or, is a sample of ELL students biased because it includes only individuals whose first language is Spanish, Tagalog, Chinese or another of the most spoken languages in the US but leaves out individuals from other linguistic groups? The ways in which factors such as ethnicity, language background, and socioeconomic status are defined and understood shape the extent to which samples are truly representative of a population.

While some educators may perceive the notion of sampling as relevant only to large-scale testing, it is also important in the classroom context, especially in formative assessment activities (Ruiz-Primo, 2013). An example from the perspective of formative assessment illustrates why this notion is related to fairness in the classroom:

> Every now and then, throughout her teaching of a lesson, a teacher poses a question to the class to gauge understanding of concepts that she knows are challenging to her students. The information she obtains allows her to adjust her teaching, for example, by discussing certain concepts in more detail. When nobody raises their hand, she calls the names of specific students and asks them to respond to her questions.

This teacher's questioning can be viewed as drawing samples of students to inform her teaching. How effectively her teaching is informed by her students' answers depends on the extent to which all her students are represented in these samples. Throughout the lesson, does she include all students (e.g. both low- and high-achieving, both ELL and non-ELL, and both male and female students)? Or does she promote the participation of only a few? If her samples are biased, then her teaching will privilege the students based on whose answers her teaching is informed. Her teaching will be biased, as well, in the sense that it will address the needs of those few students.

The notion of sample provides a perspective for understanding how tests are constructed and, ultimately, for judging the two basic properties of tests— reliability and validity. A test can be viewed as a sample of observations. These observations consist of items, judgments from raters, occasions in which students are given the tests, and the like. Based on those observations, generalizations are made about the students' knowledge and skills in a given domain.

Validity

Validity can be defined as an evaluative judgment of the extent to which proper generalizations about students' knowledge and skills in a given domain can be made based on the scores from a test (Messick, 1989). Strictly speaking, validity does not refer to an intrinsic property of a test; rather, it refers to the quality of interpretations of the information obtained from that test. The statement that a test "is valid" or produces "valid measures" should always be accompanied by information of the population for which the instrument was created (Geisinger, 1998). Otherwise, the statement may mislead to thinking that the instrument's validity is a property that is preserved under any circumstance. As a rule, it is always recommendable to refer to the validity of interpretations of the scores produced by a test, rather than the validity of a test.

Because a test is a sample of a given domain of knowledge and skills, arguments in favor or against the validity of a test can be constructed based on how representative the sample is of that domain. For example, are the situations, problems, and questions included in the test representative of the situations and problems that define that domain? Are the knowledge and skills needed to solve the problems and situations included in a test relevant to the construct being measured?

Evidence of validity can be examined in multiple ways (Note 1.1). For example, the performance of students who are known to have the skills being measured can be compared with the performance of students who are known to not have those skills. Or, the performance of students on the test being evaluated can be compared with the performance of the same students on another test intended to measure the same or a similar construct and with the performance of those students on another test intended to measure a very different construct. Appropriate judgments on validity should be based on different pieces of evidence. This is especially the case in the testing of ELL students, in which proficiency in the language in which tests are administered is frequently confounded with the constructs measured.

Reliability

While *validity* refers to the accuracy with which a test, as a sample of observations, represents a domain of knowledge and skills, *reliability* refers to the sufficiency of those observations (Shavelson & Webb, 2009). The performance of students varies across items that measure the same construct. It also varies across occasions, even if the items used to test the students on different occasions are the same. Also, for students' responses whose assessment requires human judgment, the performance of the same students on the same task may be perceived differently by different raters.

Reliability can be defined as the consistency of measures of academic achievement across observations in the judgment of student performance (see Haertel, 2006). This consistency has different facets, depending on the characteristics of the test. For example, it may refer to the consistency of scores across different subsets of items in a test (internal consistency), or the consistency of the judgments made by different raters (inter-rater reliability), or the consistency of the scores obtained by the students on the same task across different testing occasions (stability).

Fairness

Fairness is the term used to refer to the ability of tests and testing practices to produce information that is not influenced by students' personal characteristics such as gender, race, ethnicity, and first language, and which are not part of what is being measured. Since these personal factors are irrelevant to the constructs measured, fairness is an aspect of validity (Messick, 1989). Yet listing validity and fairness separately stresses the fact that, often, issues of validity ultimately have an adverse impact on the performance on tests of segments of the population historically underrepresented in a society.

To a large extent, fairness has to do with differences in the sets of cultural experiences beyond the school between racial, cultural, and linguistic groups, and gender groups. Many items in tests provide contexts (situations, scenarios, stories, and fictitious characters) intended to make the problems they pose meaningful to students' everyday life experiences. While these contexts are assumed to be shared by all students, they may reflect the life style, values, and socioeconomic status of certain groups. While the impact of this marginalization on student performance in tests is yet to be investigated, a wealth of literature with students from different cultural groups documents the importance that instruction be sensitive to the students' cultural experiences (e.g. Brisk, 2006; Delpit, 1995; Ladson-Billings, 2002; Lipka, Sharp, Adams, & Sharp, 2007).

A common misconception about fairness in testing is that it is possible to create items that are culture-free, in the sense that they do not reflect any specific culture. In actuality, tests and testing practices are cultural products and they necessarily reflect the characteristics of the societies that generate them (Cole, 1999). Ensuring the participation of individuals with diverse cultural backgrounds in the process of test development is one of the actions usually taken with the intent to ensure fairness. Ideally, also students with diverse multiple cultural backgrounds should be included throughout the entire process of test development.

Another common misconception about fairness is that if students from a given group perform lower than students from another group on an item or test, then the item or the test is unfair. In actuality, there are cases in which two groups perform differently because a genuine difference in the knowledge and skill between the two groups exists.

Issues of fairness can be addressed through the use of analytical procedures (e.g. Camilli & Shepard, 1994) that allow detection of biased items—items in which students from two groups perform differently after differences in the overall levels of achievement are controlled for. However, these procedures may not be sufficient to ensure fairness and are unlikely to be used routinely to scrutinize all the items included in a given test.

Closing Comments

Assessment involves integrating and evaluating information on student academic achievement from different sources. Proper sampling is critical to ensuring that that information is relevant and sufficient to making sound evaluative judgments. Sampling concerns validity, reliability, and fairness.

A sampling perspective allows examination of the quality of testing practices performed by assessment systems, test developers, and educators. Among others, aspects of these testing practices include: determining the content of a test and the kinds of items it should include; determining the appropriate number of items in a test; ensuring the participation of students with different cultural backgrounds throughout different stages of the process of test development; and, in the context of classroom assessment, collecting information from all students during instruction to have a sense of their understanding and progress towards certain instructional goals.

While sampling is relevant to valid and fair testing for all students, sampling issues are particularly important in the assessment of ELL students. Because ELL populations are complex and heterogeneous, their characteristics may not be properly taken into consideration and, therefore, they may not be properly represented in the process of assessment. Possible cases of underrepresentation are: certain students are wrongly included or excluded from different categories of English proficiency; certain linguistic groups of ELLs (e.g. native users of different languages) are treated as if they were the same; ELL students are not included in samples of pilot students to try out and refine the wording of items; and, in the classroom, ELL students may not be properly included in instructional and assessment activities.

Attention to sampling and awareness of its importance in both large-scale and classroom assessment help educators to be critical users of tests and to improve and evaluate their own assessment practices.

Exercises

Exercise 1.1: Formative Assessment, Teaching, and Sampling

1. Discuss the value of formative assessment as a teaching resource.
    *   What do the Socratic method, described as "teaching by asking, not simply telling," and the notion of formative assessment as assessment for learning have in common?
    *   How can assessment, as a method of inquiry, contribute to promoting critical thinking skills among your students?
    *   Can a task used in large-scale assessment also be used as a formative assessment task? Justify your answer and provide examples.
2. Reflect on your formative assessment practices using the perspective of sampling. What actions do you take to insure that you take into consideration all your students to inform your teaching?

Exercise 1.2: Construct

1. Visit the website of your state's assessment system. Find, in the sample of released items, three items for the grade you teach.
2. Create two alternative forms of the same items. For example, if an item is a multiple-choice, create an open-ended version of the item.
3. Reflect on the following issues:
    *   Can different forms of the same item measure the same construct? Are the reasoning and skills needed to respond correctly to the different forms of items the same? Why?

- What are the ways in which changes of wording, appearance, and context may influence the constructs measured by items?
- How do the different forms of items vary as to the sets of linguistic challenges they may pose to students?

Exercise 1.3: Test Content and Sampling

1. Select a topic from the subject and grade you teach and pretend you need to write a test consisting of only ten items to assess your students' knowledge of the topic.
   - Using the notion of sampling and your state's standards document on the corresponding content area, how would you select the content of the items to be included to ensure proper content representation?
   - Since different types of items pose different types of linguistic demands, what sampling actions would you take to minimize the effect on student performance of language demands that are not relevant to the constructs measured?
2. Based on the notion of sampling, discuss:
   - Why do tests usually contain more than one item?
   - What are three ways in which fairness and sampling are related?
   - Why is sampling particularly important to take into account in the testing of ELL populations?

Exercise 1.4: Information from Assessment Systems

1. Discuss the information provided by large-scale assessment systems regarding content knowledge.
   - What kind of information do you receive from your state's assessment system about your students' academic achievement?
   - What kinds of difficulties do you experience interpreting this information?
   - What actions do you think you should take to make sure that the information provided by your state's assessment system helps you to improve your teaching?
   - What kind of feedback would you give to your state's assessment system, so that your teaching benefits more from the information it provides on student academic achievement?
2. Discuss the information provided by large-scale assessment systems regarding your ELL students' English proficiency.
   - What kind of information do you receive from your state's assessment system about your ELL students' proficiency in English?
   - What kinds of difficulties do you experience interpreting this information?

- What actions do you think you should take to make sure that the information provided by your state's assessment system helps you to support your ELL students more effectively?
- What kind of feedback would you give to your state's assessment system, so that you can support your ELL students more effectively based on the information it provides on their proficiency in English?

Note

Note 1.1. Validity issues are discussed throughout the book, rather than in a separate chapter, in relation to multiple aspects of ELL assessment. Still, forms of validity evidence based on content and on response process are addressed specifically in Chapter 8 in relation to test review activities; also, forms of validity evidence based on the relations of test scores to other variables are discussed in Chapter 9, which focuses on the quantifiable attributes of tests.

References

Abedi, J., Hofstetter, C., & Lord, C. (2004). Assessment accommodations for English language learners: Implications for policy-based empirical research. *Review of Educational Research, 74*(1), 1–28.

Arter, J. (1999). Teaching about performance assessment. *Educational Measurement: Issues and Practice, 18*(2), 30–44.

Arter, J. & McTighe, J. (2000). *Scoring rubrics in the classroom*. (2000). Thousand Oaks, CA: Corwin Press.

Baxter, G. P., Shavelson, R. J., Goldman, S. R., & Pine, J. (1992). Evaluation of procedure-based scoring for hands-on science assessment. *Journal of Educational Measurement, 29*(1), 1–17.

Black, P. & Wiliam, D. (2009). Developing the theory of formative assessment. *Educational Assessment, Evaluation and Accountability, 21*, 5–21.

Brisk, M. E. (2006). *Bilingual education: From compensatory to quality schooling* (2nd ed.). Mahwah, NJ: Lawrence Erlbaum Associates, Publishers.

Camilli, G. (2006). Test fairness. In R. L. Brennan (Ed.), *Educational measurement* (4th ed.) (pp. 221–256). Westport, CT: American Council on Education and Praeger Publishers.

Camilli, G. & Shepard, L. (1994). *Methods for identifying biased test items*. Thousands Oaks, CA: Sage.

Cole, M. (1999). Culture-free versus culture-based measures of cognition. In R. J. Sternberg (Ed.), *The nature of cognition* (pp. 645–664). Cambridge, MA: The MIT Press.

Cook, L. I. & Schmitt-Cascallar, A. P. (2005). Establishing score comparability for tests given in different languages. In R. K. Hambleton, P. F. Merenda, & C. D. Spielberger (Eds.), *Adapting educational and psychological tests for cross-cultural assessment* (pp. 139–169). Mahwah, NJ: Lawrence Erlbaum Associates, Publishers.

Crocker, L., & Algina, J. (2008). *Introduction to classical and modern test theory*. Mason, OH: Cengage Learning.

Cronbach, L. J. (1990). *Essentials of psychological testing, 5th edition*. New York: Harper & Row, Publishers, Inc.

Delpit, L. (1995). *Other people's children: Cultural conflict in the classroom*. New York: New Press.

Feldt, L. S. & Brennan, R. L. (1989). Reliability. In R. L. Linn (Ed.), *Educational measurement* (3rd ed.) (pp. 105–146). Washington, DC: American Council on Education & National Council on Measurement in Education.

García, O., Kleifgen, A., & Falchi, L. (2008). *From English language learners to emergent bilinguals*. Equity Matters: Research Review No. 1.

Geisinger, K. F. (1998). Psychometric issues in test interpretation. In J. Sandoval, C. L. Frisby, K. F. Geisinger, J. D. Scheuneman, & J. R. Grenier (Eds.), *Test interpretation and diversity: Achieving equity in assessment*. Washington, DC: American Psychological Association.

Haertel, E. H. (2006). Reliability. In R. L. Brennan (Ed.), *Educational measurement* (4th ed.) (pp. 65–110). Westport, CT: American Council on Education and Praeger Publishers.

Hakuta, K. (2000). *How long does it take English learners to attain proficiency?* University of California Linguistic Minority Research Institute. Policy Reports. Santa Barbara: Linguistic Minority Research Institute. Retrieved July 28, 2009 from http://repositories.cdlib.org/lmri/pr/hakuta.

Heath, S. B. (1983). *Ways with words: Language, life and work in communities and classrooms*. Cambridge, UK: Cambridge University Press.

Kane, M. (2006). Content-related validity evidence in test development. In S. M. Downing & T. M. Haladyna (Eds.), *Handbook of test development* (pp. 131–153). Mahwah, NJ: Lawrence Erlbaum Associates, Publishers.

Ladson-Billings, G. (2002). But that's just good teaching! The case for culturally relevant pedagogy. *Theory into Practice, 34*(3), 159–165.

Lipka, J., Sharp, N., Adams, B., & Sharp, F. (2007). Creating a third space for authentic biculturalism: Examples from math in a cultural context. *Journal of American Indian Education, 46*(3), 94–115.

Martinez, M. E. (1999). Cognition and the question of test item format. *Educational Psychologist, 34*(4), 207–218.

Mazzeo, J., Lazer, S., & Zieky, M. J. (2006). Monitoring educational progress with group-score assessments. In R. L. Brennan (Ed.), *Educational measurement* (4th ed.) (pp. 681–699). Westport, CT: American Council on Education and Praeger Publishers.

Messick, S. (1989). Validity. In R. L. Linn (Ed.), *Educational measurement* (3rd ed.) (pp. 13–103). Washington, DC: American Council on Education & National Council on Measurement in Education.

Mlodinov, I. (2008). *The drunkard's walk: How randomness rules our lives.* New York: Pantheon Books.

Morgan, C. (1998). *Writing mathematically: The discourse investigation.* London: Falmer Press.

National Center for Education Statistics (2011). *National Assessment of Educational Progress (NAEP):* Retrieved April 8, 2011 from http://nces.ed.gov/nationsreportcard/about/.

Pedhazur, E. J. & Pedhazur-Schmelkin, L. (1991). *Measurement, design, and analysis: An integrated approach.* Hillsdale, NJ: Lawrence Erlbaum Associates, Publishers.

Pellegrino, J. W., Chudowsky, N., & Glaser, R. (2001). *Knowing what students know: The science and design of educational assessment.* Washington, DC: National Academy Press.

Pimm, C. (1987). *Speaking mathematically: Communication in mathematics classrooms.* London: Routledge & Kegan Paul Ltd.

Raizen, S. A. (1997). *Standards for science education.* Occasional Paper No. 1. Madison, WI: National Institute for Science Education, University of Wisconsin–Madison and National Center for Improving Science Education.

Ruiz-Primo, M. A. (2013, April). Formative assessment in multilingual classrooms. Keynote Address. *Center for Culturally Responsive Evaluation and Assessment Inaugural Conference.* Chicago: University of Illinois at Urbana–Champaign.

Shavelson, R. J. & Webb, N. M. (2009). Generalizability theory and its contribution to the discussion of the generalizability of research findings. In K. Ercikan & W. -M. Roth (Eds.), *Generalizing from educational research: Beyond qualitative and quantitative polarization* (pp. 13–31). New York: Routledge.

Sireci, S. G. & Zenisky. (2006). Innovative item formats in computer-based testing: In pursuit of improved construct presentation. In S. M. Downing & T. M. Haladyna (Eds.), *Handbook of test development* (pp. 329–347). Mahwah, NJ: Lawrence Erlbaum Associates, Publishers.

Snow, C. (2010). Academic language and the challenge of reading and learning about science. *Science, 328,* 450–452.

Solano-Flores, G. & Trumbull, E. (2008). In what language should English language learners be tested? In R. J. Kopriva (Ed.), *Improving testing for English language learners: A comprehensive approach to designing, building, implementing and interpreting better academic assessments* (pp. 169–200). New York: Routledge.

Wilson, M. R. & Bertenthal, M.W. (Eds.) (2006). *Systems for state science assessment.* Committee on Test Design for K–12 Science Achievement, Board on Testing and Assessment, Center for Education, Division of Behavioral and Social Sciences and Education. National Research Council of the National Academies. Washington, DC: The National Academies Press.

2

LANGUAGE, ASSESSMENT, AND ENGLISH LANGUAGE LEARNERS

Overview

This chapter examines important concepts and ideas from the language sciences (mainly from the fields of sociolinguistics and language development) that are critical to properly addressing language issues in the assessment of ELL students.

The section "Language as a System" provides a functional perspective according to which languages are systems of conventions. The section "Assessment as a Communication Process" provides a conceptual perspective according to which testing and classroom assessment activities involve social interaction through language.

The section "Understanding English Language Learners" discusses how these students' linguistic skills are commonly underappreciated. When considered together, the skills of ELL students in both English and their first language reflect the development of a sophisticated, complex language system.

The section "Language Variation" discusses how individuals and groups vary in the ways in which they use the same language. Facets of this variation include the diversity of dialects in the same language, diverse forms of specialized language such as academic language, and code-switching.

Language as a System

For the purpose of this book, a *language* can be thought of as a system of conventions shared by the members of a society to communicate and make meaning in four language modes—listening, speaking, reading, and writing. Listening and reading are typically referred to as *reception modes* whereas speaking and writing are referred to as *production modes*.

In the definition, the term *convention* refers to the fact that the multiple features of a language (pronunciation, spelling, vocabulary, grammatical structure, style, and discourse, among many others) are arbitrary, not determined by nature. The features of a language are socially constructed, agreed upon, and transmitted (Wardhaugh, 2002). For example, the use of the ending *ed* as a marker of past tense in many English verbs (regular verbs) is a convention in the sense that it is arbitrary. There is no correspondence between *ed* and the nature of an event or action that took place in the past; any other marker could denote past tense. The marker *ed* conveys a specific meaning in English because it is consistently attached to verbs that describe actions or events that took place in the past. The exceptions to this rule are also conventions, as is the case in which past time is denoted for irregular verbs such as *eat*, *can*, and *take*.

The majority of these conventions evolve with time; they are not created deliberately by design. Linguists have been able to examine patterns in which languages evolve. For example, irregular verbs in English tend to disappear—a process that has been occurring over centuries. The least frequently used irregular verbs are the most likely to become regular; the most frequently used irregular verbs are the least likely to become regular (Lieberman, Michel, Jackson, Tang, & Nowak, 2007).

In the definition of language provided above, the term *system* refers to the fact that all the components of the language function coherently as a whole. Because a language is a system, it is possible to express same or similar ideas in multiple ways. See the four utterances below:

> I think I should be going.
> It is time for me to leave.
> I'd rather be going.
> Time for me to hit the road.

Each utterance uses a particular combination of conventions concerning vocabulary, verbs, contractions, idiomatic expressions, styles, and other features. Yet all of them are consistent with the conventions used in English. All convey approximately the same meaning, in terms of the actions or intentions described. But they vary slightly in the way in which they convey that meaning in combination, express different levels of formality, different emotional tones, and different assumed levels of familiarity with the interlocutor. The appropriateness of utterances like these in different social contexts is also governed by a system of conventions shared by a community of users of a language (see Halliday, 1978).

Common sense leads to thinking about different languages as clearly distinguishable entities. For example, French and English are thought of and referred to as two different languages. Yet while, conceptually, they are separate categories, they share many attributes. For example, they share a common ancestry, their grammars are similar (e.g. sentences are typically constructed in a sequence in the order Subject–Verb–Object, as in *[I]–[want]–[a glass of water]*), they have many phonemes (sounds) in common, they have the same alphabetic writing system, and they share many expressions that they have borrowed from each other (e.g. *pork, fiancé, hors d'oeuvres, baguette*).

Assessment as a Communication Process

Language is the medium through which assessment takes place. So much so, that it is widely recognized that, at least to some extent, tests unintentionally assess proficiency in the language in which they are administered (AERA, APA, NCME, 2014). In large-scale assessment, limited proficiency in the language in which tests are administered is a major potential threat to fairness in testing and to the validity of the interpretations of test scores. In the classroom context, limited proficiency in the language of instruction not only prevents ELL students from benefitting from instruction; it also prevents teachers from obtaining, through classroom assessment activities, appropriate information about their ELL students' learning.

The majority of assessment activities entail a communication process or some form of social interaction (Solano-Flores, 2008). For example, in formal classroom assessment, a test provides directions for students to know what is expected from them and asks questions which students need to answer; and the teacher interprets the students' responses to the questions. Or, during classroom conversations, the teacher develops a sense of the level of progress of their students, their misconceptions, their preferences, and their cognitive styles, among many other things. Also, the teacher has the opportunity to provide feedback that helps students to identify areas of improvement in their learning.

This process of communication or social interaction may fail when students cannot understand the questions they are being asked or are not able to express their responses to those questions. It also may fail when teachers are not able to ask questions in ways that are comprehensible to all students or when they are not able to make accurate interpretations of what some students say. Also, this process of communication or social interaction may fail when teachers have inaccurate perceptions of their students' communication skills. For example, a teacher may underestimate the ability of certain ELL students to communicate in English and may not include them in classroom conversations, guided by the wrong premise that they cannot participate in such conversations. This flawed communication process limits the opportunities offered to ELL students to benefit from instruction.

The view of assessment as a communication process underscores the need for properly understanding the needs and capabilities of ELL students (Durán, 2008). Labels such as "non-English proficient" or "limited English proficient" or a score on a test of English as a second language are useful for school districts and states to make classification decisions. However, such labels do not provide educators with the level of information they need to properly assess their ELL students and support their learning through classroom assessment. Thus, in order to be able to properly assess their ELL students, it is important for educators to understand what defines an ELL student, and what, exactly, English proficiency is.

Understanding English Language Learners

English Language Learners as Emergent Bilinguals

For the purposes of this book, English language learners (ELLs) are defined as students whose first language is not English and who are developing English as an additional language while they continue developing their first language. The term *emergent bilingual* has been proposed as an alternative term to replace the term *English language learner* (García, Kleifgen, & Falchi, 2008). Since the transition in the use of terms in the education parlance is still in progress, both terms are used in this book indistinctly.

The use of the term *emergent bilingual* implies a view of bilingualism as an asset, not a deficit. Viewing ELLs as emergent bilinguals allows proper consideration of the fact that, cognitively, bilingual individuals develop a rich and complex system that integrates their first and second languages coherently (Cummins, 2000).

Distorted views of the capacities of ELLs are produced when the fact that they are developing two languages is not properly taken into account. A well-established notion among language development and bilingualism professionals is that bilinguals are not two separate monolinguals (Grosjean, 1989). Understanding this notion is important for educators to have accurate expectations about the potential of their ELL students, even if they do not have information about the proficiency of these students in their first language.

Language Proficiency

Measures from language proficiency tests provide educators with initial information on the level of English development of their ELL students. However, these measures should be used judiciously. First, it should always be kept in mind that proficiency in a language is a complex construct that involves many skills (Durán, 1989). Second, as discussed in Chapter 1, tests are samples of domains of knowledge and skills. The tasks included in language proficiency tests are samples of the myriads of instances and situations in which language is used. As such, there is a limit to the extent to which they capture the complexity of these students' linguistic repertoires. Because language proficiency is a tremendously vast domain, a given student may be classified above or below their actual level of English proficiency simply because the items and tasks in the test cannot reflect all the contexts in which that student uses English. Two given students with comparable proficiencies may be classified at different levels of proficiency, or two given students with different proficiencies may be classified at the same level of proficiency.

Having a clear idea of the limitations of language proficiency tests and the measures they produce enables educators to develop practices that ensure their proper use. Three main practices can be identified. The first practice consists of using measures of English proficiency as sources that inform teaching decisions. For example, knowing the levels of proficiency at which different ELL students are classified allows devising the level of individualized instruction intended to ensure have equal opportunities to learn.

The second practice consists of using measures from different tests in combination to make decisions about each ELL student's level of English proficiency. This practice is supported by a well-established notion that different tests that intend to measure the same construct are not necessarily exchangeable (Baxter & Shavelson, 1994; Rosenquist, Shavelson, & Ruiz-Primo, 2000). Language proficiency tests tend to focus on different aspects of language and have different kinds of items (García, McKoon, & August, 2006). Thinking about the extent to and the ways in which measures from different tests present similar or different pictures of the English proficiency of a given student allows for developing a sophisticated understanding of their strengths and skills.

The third practice consists of creating multiple opportunities to interact with ELL students and develop, based on those interactions, an independent judgment of their proficiency in English. It is through the inclusion of ELLs in all classroom activities and the direct interaction with their ELL students that educators can develop a sense of how they can communicate with them. Underlying this practice is a comprehensive view of language proficiency based on communicative competence. *Communicative competence* includes not only the knowledge of the grammatical forms of a language (e.g. phonology, morphology, syntax, vocabulary) but also the functions of language (e.g. expressing feelings, showing disagreement, asking a favor) under various social contexts (see Bachman, 2002; Canale & Swain, 1980; Hymes, 1972; Trumbull & Farr, 2005).

A mistake educators can make in the way they relate to ELLs consists of interpreting the label of "ELL" as an absolute lack of English proficiency, which leads to not attempting to interact with them. This mistake unintentionally leads to isolation and prevents educators from developing their own judgment of their students' proficiency in English. Hesitation to interact with ELLs may be more likely to occur among teachers who are monolingual, native English speakers, and who may feel that they lack the resources needed to socialize with them. Fortunately, there is evidence that indicates that the majority of ELL students have a set of basic communication skills that allows them to interact in English with their peers and teachers (Prosser & Solano-Flores, 2010). This set of skills can be the starting point for relating to ELL students and developing a good sense of their proficiency in English.

Language Variation

Dialect

Common sense leads to thinking about languages as fixed and static. Yet, there is variation within a language. Two concepts relevant to language variation are of special interest in the assessment of ELL students. Poor understanding of these concepts may misguide teaching and assessment practices. These concepts are dialect and register.

Dialects are mostly mutually intelligible varieties of the same language that differ on features such as pronunciation, vocabulary, the use of idiomatic expressions, and discursive forms, among many other attributes (Wolfram, Adger, & Christian, 1999). Dialects are associated to the combination of factors such as social group, geographical region, and socioeconomic status. They are the result of social distance, social stratification, and cultural differences.

While the term *dialect* is sometimes used to characterize the variety of a language as corrupted, low class, or poorly developed, the use of any language necessarily implies the use of a dialect of that language. Indeed, everybody necessarily speaks or writes in the dialects of a language when they use that language. Even the most prestigious variety of a language is a dialect. *Standard English* is the term used to refer to the socially prestigious variety of English predominantly used in books and the media. The perception of the standard dialect of a language as more correct and logical than other, non-standard dialects is a result of its association with power and social prestige (Coulmas, 2013). This erroneous perception may affect how student users of certain dialects are viewed—for example, as unable to think logically. In actuality, even the less prestigious dialects in a society are sophisticated systems of conventions established through patterned use (Wolfram, Adger, & Christian, 1999).

While dialects are mutually intelligible varieties of a language, familiarity with and exposure to a given dialect influences the ease with which an individual uses it. This can be especially the case among young children, who, for example, may not be used to the words, terms, and idiomatic expressions used in the classroom or in tests (Delpit, 1995). Tests are administered in the standard dialect of a language (either English, or the ELL students' first language) because that standard dialect is socially acceptable, but they should not be assumed to be written in a dialect with which everybody is equally familiar (Solano-Flores, 2006). The difference is not trivial—there is evidence that the performance of ELL students tested in their native language is sensitive to variations in the dialect of that language used in tests (Solano-Flores & Li, 2009).

Register

Strictly speaking, *academic language* is a *register*, a concept from the field of sociolinguistics used to refer to a form of specialized language (see Schleppegrell, 2004). Unlike dialect, which is a reflection of culture, identity, and social differentiation, register is a result of human activity, context, and specialization (Halliday, 1978). The variety of languages used by lawyers in their profession is frequently used as an example of a register. However, registers are not restricted to professions. Registers develop in ways that meet the communication needs of groups or communities engaged in common endeavors. This applies to any human activity, from the most despised to the most prestigious activities.

Academic language is the register that has been developed and is used in the context of academic disciplines such as mathematics, science, or history. Academic language is the register used in printed material on those disciplines, such as specialized journals and textbooks. Also, it is the register used in schools and classrooms to teach and assess knowledge on those disciplines (Bailey & Butler, 2003; Scarcella, 2003).

Whereas it is typically associated with the technical terminology of a discipline, there is much more to academic language than words or vocabulary. Academic language also involves ways of building arguments, expressing agreement or disagreement, or asking questions, among other skills (Schleppegrell, 2004). Developing academic language entails developing a sophisticated style of communicating and socializing. While ELLs can develop basic communication skills in a relatively short time after they are schooled in English, it may take several years to develop the academic language needed to benefit from instruction in English (Hakuta, Butler, & Witt, 2000). Critical to the development of academic language in ELL students is the teacher's ability to create a safe environment and promote socialization processes that enable these students to be active participants in all classroom activities (Del Rosal, 2015). Also critical is for these students to be given the opportunity to use academic language in meaningful ways (Lee, Quinn, & Valdés, 2013).

Based on the notion that developing academic language takes much longer than developing everyday language, efforts to fairly assess ELLs are sometimes oriented to minimizing the academic language demands of items. The intent is to simplify the linguistic features of items by rephrasing them in plain language. While well intentioned, those efforts may be limited in their effectiveness to make the items more accessible to ELLs. There are several reasons. One is that the register of a discipline evolves along with the advances of that discipline to meet the communication needs of its community. As a consequence, the academic language of a discipline cannot be separated from the knowledge it encodes. Learning the content of a discipline involves, to a large extent, learning the language used in that discipline. In turn, the academic language of a discipline is, to a large extent, a means through which that discipline is taught and learned.

Another reason is that ELL students whose schooling history is only in English may not be as likely to gain access to rephrased items as they are when those items keep the academic language in which they have received instruction. Furthermore, because academic language is highly encoded, rephrasing it often requires the use of many or long phrases or sentences. Attempting to minimize the academic language load of items may increase their reading demands.

The boundary between academic language and natural (everyday) language is fuzzy. So much so, that some authors claim that the distinction between natural language and academic language is a false dichotomy (O'Halloran, 2005) that may mislead educators into ignoring natural language and everyday discursive practices as valuable resources from which disciplinary knowledge and academic language can be constructed (Gutiérrez, Sengupta-Irving, & Dieckmann, 2010).

It appears fair to say that what counts and what does not count as academic language is a matter of degree and is shaped by the context in which certain terms, expressions, discursive forms, or other constituents are used (Wellington & Osborne, 2001). For example, some constituents may be used in both natural language and in a discipline (e.g. *nevertheless, in contrast*), but they may be more frequently used in the context of that discipline than in other contexts. Also, some constituents that are used in both natural language and in the academic language of a discipline may have different meanings (e.g. *mass, matter*). Due to these complexities, developing the academic language needed to learn the content of a discipline is a challenging process for any student. The process is even more challenging for ELL students because, unlike their non-ELL counterparts, they do not have a fully developed natural English language that can support the development of their academic language in English (Solano-Flores, Barnett-Clarke, & Kachchaf, 2013).

Modern views of academic language not only question the dichotomy of academic and everyday language; they also promote an integrated view of the multiple forms in which knowledge and meaning is represented in the disciplines. From a semiotic perspective, oral and written forms of language are among the many modalities in which meaning is conveyed. According to this view, being proficient in a discipline entails being able to both convey and make meaning through multiple *semiotic resources* according to social conventions specific to the discipline (Kress, 2010; Lemke, 1998; O'Halloran, 2011; Schleppegrell, 2010). These semiotic resources include, among many others, words, discursive forms, and other verbal and textual modalities. They also include graphs, formulas, charts, pictures, diagrams, and other forms of representation to convey or make meaning.

This semiotic perspective allows examination of the complex interaction of language and disciplinary knowledge. Learning cannot take place without developing the skill to represent information and understand representations of that information through multiple semiotic modalities (including language) according to social conventions.

Code-Switching

A phenomenon commonly observed among bilingual individuals is *code-switching*—a behavior consisting of alternating between two languages during conversation. This alternation can take place between sentences or even within one sentence.

Code-switching has been investigated extensively among bilinguals who speak different combinations of languages (Poplack, 2002; Romaine, 1995). Evidence from that research shows consistently that, rather than a reflection of deficit, code-switching is a reflection of an ability. A proof of that ability is that code-switchers are able to construct sentences that combine their two languages without violating the grammatical rules of either one of them. This ability indeed supports the notion that bilinguals develop a language system that integrates their two languages. This system allows them to identify commonalities and differences in the structural properties that their two languages have in common. This is good news for educators, who might fear their ELL students are confused when they observe them using two languages in combination.

A common misconception about code-switching is that it may hamper or delay the development of the second language. Contrary to this misconception, there is no evidence that using their first language hampers the development of their second language (Crystal, 1997). Code-switching can be seen as serving a communication function. Bilingual individuals may use one language or another depending on how effectively each language allows them to express feelings, make computations, or build an argument, among many other functions (Romaine, 1995). When a bilingual individual switches from one language to another is shaped by many factors, including the person's level of proficiency in each language, the level of proficiency of the interlocutor in each language, the topic of conversation, the social context (e.g. the presence of monolingual or other bilinguals), and even the set of affordances and constraints of each language to express certain ideas.

Closing Comments

Misconceptions concerning language proficiency, dialect, and code-switching affect the accuracy with which teachers perceive the linguistic and intellectual competencies of their ELL students. Awareness of these misconceptions is essential to validly and fairly assessing these students' academic achievement.

Critical to properly teaching and assessing ELL students is the notion that these students are developing proficiency in two languages, not one. The linguistic resources of ELL students and their intellectual abilities are underestimated when this double challenge is not taken into consideration.

Proficiency in a second language is not absolute. What counts as proficiency in English as a second language is shaped by the context in which language is used. Thus, while valuable, the information on language proficiency produced by English proficiency tests should be used in combination with other sources of information.

To effectively support their ELL students, educators need to use information from tests of English proficiency along with other, formal and informal sources of information about the proficiency of their ELL students in English. Social interaction is a basic condition for effective assessment. If this interaction is not effective, assessment cannot produce accurate information about the students' academic achievement and cannot effectively inform teachers' instructional decisions. Social interaction with each of their ELL students is necessary for educators to have a sense of each of their ELL students' proficiency in English and to devise optimal ways in which they can support their learning.

Exercises

Exercise 2.1: Knowing Individual ELL Students' Proficiency in English

1. Select three ELL students, A, B, and C. Using the format shown in Figure 2.1, briefly describe, in the corresponding cell, each of the student's skills in English in different language modalities.

   Be specific in your descriptions. This example illustrates the kind of description you need to provide in each cell, regarding oral communication:

   > *The student is able to sustain a conversation on different topics, although she is still unfamiliar with some colloquial words and idiomatic expressions. While she makes mistakes with verb tenses and conjugation, she communicates ideas efficiently.*

2. Write your descriptions in ways in which you can identify commonalities and differences in the three students' proficiency in English.
3. Make sure that your descriptions are based on your experiences interacting with the students. Do not use information from tests or students' self-reports.
4. When you finish filling out the table, reflect about the experience examining the commonalities and differences in the students' proficiency in English:
   - How difficult or easy was it for you to provide information on the students' proficiency in English?
   - What did you learn about the differences and commonalities in your students' proficiency in English?
   - In terms of quality and clarity, how is the information you gathered about your students' proficiency in English different from information provided by tests?

	Student A	Student B	Student C
Oral Communication (Listening and Speaking)			
Reading			
Writing			

FIGURE 2.1 Format for reporting commonalities and differences in the proficiency in English of three students.

Exercise 2.2: Social Interaction with ELL Students

1. Use the format shown in Figure 2.2 to keep a log of the individual interactions you have with your ELL students during one week. Record at least five interactions per day.
2. Record the day and time of each individual interaction, the name of the student, and the description of the interaction. In your description of each interaction, make sure to describe:
    *   the context in which the interaction originated (e.g. the lesson you were teaching and the activities in which the class was engaged when the interaction took place);
    *   whether you or the student initiated the interaction;
    *   the communicative function of the interaction (e.g. clarify a concept, ask a question, give or interpret directions, discuss a topic, ask a question, complain about something); and
    *   any comments about what you have learned about the student's skills.
3. Do not wait too much time for the students to initiate the interactions. You may need to initiate the majority of the interactions. Make sure you report interactions with different ELL students.
4. At the end of the week, examine your log and reflect about your interaction with ELL students:
    *   How frequent were your interactions at the beginning of the week and how frequent were they at the end of the week? Why?
    *   What did you learn about your ELL students' proficiency in English that you were not aware of?

Day, Time	Student	Description of the Interaction

FIGURE 2.2 Format for the log of individual interactions with ELL students.

References

American Educational Research Association, American Psychological Association, and National Council for Measurement in Education (2014). *Standards for Educational and Psychological Testing.* Washington, DC: Author.

Bachman, L. F. (2002). Alternative interpretations of alternative assessments: Some validity issues in educational performance assessments. *Journal of Educational Measurement, 2*(13), 5–18.

Bailey, A. L. & Butler, F. A. (2003). *An evidentiary framework for operationalizing academic language for broad application to K–12 education: A design document.* (CSE Tech. Rep. No. 611). Los Angeles: University of California, National Center for Research on Evaluation, Standards, and Student Testing.

Baxter, G. P. & Shavelson, R. J. (1994). Science performance assessments: Benchmarks and surrogates. *International Journal of Educational Research, 21,* 279–298.

Canale, M. & Swain, M. (1980). Theoretical bases of communicative approaches to second language teaching and testing. *Applied Linguistics, 1*(1), 1–47.

Coulmas, F. (2013). *Sociolinguistics: The study of speakers' choices. 2nd Edition.* New York: Cambridge University Press.

Crystal, D. (1997). *The Cambridge encyclopedia of language* (2nd ed.)., Cambridge, UK: Cambridge University Press.

Cummins, J. (2000). *Language, power, and pedagogy: Bilingual children in the crossfire.* Clevedon, England: Multilingual Matters Ltd.

Del Rosal, K. (2015). *Investigating informal formative assessment practices addressing emergent bilinguals' science academic language.* Doctoral dissertation. University of Colorado Boulder.

Delpit, L. (1995). *Other people's children: Cultural conflict in the classroom.* New York: New Press.

Durán, R. P. (1989). Testing of linguistic minorities. In R. Linn (Ed.), *Educational Measurement* (3rd ed.) (pp. 573–587). New York: American Council of Education, Macmillan.

Durán, R. P. (2008). Assessing English-language learners' achievement. *Review of Educational Research, 32,* 292–327.

García, G. E., McKoon, G., & August, D. (2006). Language and literacy assessment of language-minority students. In D. August & T. Shanahan (Eds.), *Developing literacy in second-language learners: report of the National Literacy Panel on Language-Minority Children and Youth* (pp. 597–626). Mahwah, NJ: Lawrence Erlbaum Associates, Inc., Publishers.

García, O., Kleifgen, A., & Falchi, L. (2008). *From English language learners to emergent bilinguals.* Equity Matters: Research Review No. 1.

Grosjean, F. (1989). Neurolinguists, beware! The bilingual is not two monolinguals in one person. *Brain and Language, 36,* 3–15.

Gutiérrez, K. D., Sengupta-Irving, T., & Dieckmann, J. (2010). Developing a mathematical vision: Mathematics as a discursive and embodied practice. In J. N. Moschkovich (Ed.), *Language and mathematics education: Multiple perspectives and directions for research* (pp. 29–71). Charlotte, NC: Information Age Publishing, Inc.

Hakuta, K., Butler, Y. G., Witt, D. (2000). *How long does it take English learners to attain proficiency?* (Policy Report 2000–1). The University of California Linguistic Minority Research Institute.

Halliday, M. A. K. (1978). *Language as social semiotic: The social interpretation of language and meaning.* London: Edward Arnold (Publishers), Ltd.

Hymes, D. (1972). On communicative competence. In J. B. Price & J. Holmes (Eds.), *Sociolinguistics* (pp. 269–293). Harmonsworth, UK: Penguin Books.

Kress, G. (2010). *Mutimodality: A social semiotic approach to contemporary communication.* New York: Routledge.

Lee, O., Quinn, H., & Valdés, G. (2013). Science and language for English language learners in relation to Next Generation Science Standards and with implications for Common Core State Standards for English Language Arts and Mathematics. *Educational Researcher, 42*(4), 223–233.

Lemke, J. L. (1998). Multiplying meaning: Visual and verbal semiotics in scientific text. In J. R. Martin & R. Veel (Eds.), *Reading science: Critical and functional perspectives on discourses of science* (pp. 87–113). New York: Routledge.

Lieberman, E., Michel, J. -B., Jackson, J., Tang, T., & Nowak, M. A. (2007). Quantifying the evolutionary dynamics of language. *Nature, 449*, 713–716.

O'Halloran, K. L. (2005). *Mathematical discourse: Language, symbolism and visual images.* Continuum International Publishing Group.

O'Halloran, K. L. (2011). *Multimodal discourse analysis.* In K. Hyland & B. Paltridge (Eds.), *Companion to Discourse.* London and New York: Continuum.

Poplack, S. (2001). Code-switching (linguistic). In N. Smelser & P. Baltes (Eds.), *International encyclopedia of the social and behavioral sciences*, Vol. 12 (pp. 2,062–2,065). Amsterdam: Elsevier Science Ltd.

Prosser, R. R. & Solano-Flores, G. (2010). *Including English language learners in the process of test development: A study on instrument linguistic adaptation for cognitive validity.* Paper presented at the Annual Conference of the National Council of Measurement in Education, Denver, Colorado, April 29–May 3.

Romaine, S. (1995). *Bilingualism, second edition.* Malden, MA: Blackwell Publishing.

Ronsenquist, A., Shavelson, R. J., & Ruiz-Primo, M. A. (2000). *On the "exchangeability" of hands-on and computer-simulated science performance assessments.* CSE Technical Report 531. Center for the Study of Evaluation National Center for Research on Evaluation, Standards, and Student Testing Graduate School of Education and Information Studies, University of California, Los Angeles.

Scarcella, R. C. (2003). *Academic English: A conceptual framework.* Report 2003–1. Santa Barbara, CA: University of California Linguistic Minority Research Institute.

Schleppegrell, M. J. (2004). *The language of schooling: A functional linguistics perspective.* Mahwah, NJ: Lawrence Erlbaum Associates.

Schleppegrell, M. J. (2010). Language in mathematics teaching and learning: A research review. In J. N. Moschkovich (Ed.), *Language and mathematics education: Multiple perspectives and directions for research* (pp. 73–112). Charlotte, NC: Information Age Publishing.

Solano-Flores, G. (2006). Language, dialect, and register: Sociolinguistics and the estimation of measurement error in the testing of English-language learners. *Teachers College Record. 108*(11), 2,354–2,379.

Solano-Flores, G. (2008). Who is given tests in what language by whom, when, and where? The need for probabilistic views of language in the testing of English language learners. *Educational Researcher, 37*(4), 189–199.

Solano-Flores, G. & Li, M. (2009). Language variation and score variation in the testing of English language learners, native Spanish speakers. *Educational Assessment, 14,* 1–15.

Solano-Flores, G., Barnett-Clarke, C., & Kachchaf, R. (2013). Semiotic structure and meaning making: The performance of English language learners on mathematics tests. *Educational Assessment 18*(3), 147–161.

Trumbull, E. & Farr, B. (2005). Introduction to language. In E. Trumbull & B. Farr (Eds.), *Language and learning: What teachers need to know* (pp. 1–32). Norwood, MA: Christopher-Gordon.

Wardhaugh, R. (2002). *An introduction to sociolinguistics,* (4th edition). Oxford, UK: Blackwell Publishing.

Wellington, J. & Osborne, J. (2001). *Language and literacy in science education.* Buckingham, UK: Open University Press.

Wolfram, W., Adger, C. T., & Christian, D. (1999). *Dialects in schools and communities.* Mahwah, NJ: Lawrence Erlbaum Associates, Publishers. Ch. 1: Language variation in the United States. pp. 1–34.

3

ASSESSMENT, COGNITION, AND CULTURE

Overview

This chapter examines cognition as a notion critical to understanding assessment and to developing effective assessment instruments and practices. The discussion uses a perspective that combines mainly knowledge from the fields of cognitive science and sociocultural theory. The perspective of cognitive science allows examination of processes such as understanding, learning, reasoning, and problem solving. Sociocultural theory allows examination of how those cognitive processes are shaped by culture and society.

Awareness of the role of cognitive processes in assessment enables educators to obtain the maximum benefit from assessment activities and information. For example, from their students' answers to oral or written questions, they may be able to determine not only if the responses are correct or incorrect but also to identify possible forms of reasoning, misconceptions, or problem solving strategies that lead the students to their incorrect responses. Given the strong relationship between language and cognition, this awareness is critical for educators to effectively assess their ELL students.

The section "Basic Notions of Cognition" discusses concepts originated from the field of cognitive science. It discusses aspects of cognitive activity that are relevant to creating meaningful assessment activities and instruments and to interpreting student performance on tests.

The section "Cognition and Culture" addresses the notion that, rather than taking place in isolation, cognitive processes are shaped by society. The section discusses how culture shapes thinking process and how culture and language shape the ways in which students interpret tests and respond to them.

The section "Assessment Activities with Focus on Cognition" explains how assessment can be used as a tool for probing understanding and informing instructional decisions beyond simply assigning grades. It also describes activities that can be conducted in the classroom to understand the cognitive processes that shape how students take tests and to improve assessment activities and test items.

Basic Notions of Cognition

It is an unfortunate fact that, due to the predominant role of high-stakes tests and accountability, assessment is seen more as a source for making grading decisions than as a potential resource for supporting students' learning and informing teachers' teaching. Because of this circumstance, educators' teaching and assessment practices may focus more on qualifying student performance as correct or incorrect and less on interpreting this performance.

Using assessment with a focus on cognition enables teachers to properly interpret student performance on test items in the benefit of instruction. *Cognition* and *cognitive processes* are terms used in this book to refer to the mental processes and activities underlying proficiency in a given knowledge domain. The terms are used in relation to mental activities such as learning, remembering, understanding, meaning making, and problem solving. These mental activities involve the ability to acquire, transform, elaborate, store, and retrieve information.

The importance of understanding cognitive processes in test taking can never be overestimated, as they are critical to properly understanding the limitations of assessment instruments. Attention to cognitive processes may reveal, for example, that the ways in which items are worded may mislead some students in their interpretations of those items (Solano-Flores & Trumbull, 2003); that opportunities to learn students have outside of the school influence their performance on standardized tests (Hamilton, Nussbaum, Kupermintz, Kerkhoven, & Snow, 1997); and that students may be able to respond correctly to items using reasoning and knowledge that is below the level of cognitive complexity they are intended to assess (Baxter, Elder, & Glaser, 1996).

Cognitive Load

Cognitive load is the term used to refer to the amount and complexity of information that a person needs to process simultaneously before being able to make sense of a situation or solve a problem. Cognitive theory establishes that this information is processed by a working memory whose capacity is limited (Sweller, 1994). Cognitive overload takes place when a problem contains more information than the amount of information this limited working memory can process simultaneously.

As with any situation or problem, test items impose a cognitive load on working memory (Solano-Flores, Shade, & Chrzanowski, 2014). The information students need to process in order to interpret test items and respond to them is not only the information inherent to the content being assessed, but also features such as the items' visual layout, wording, contextual information, and, in the case of computer-administered tests, the ways in which students need to enter their responses (e.g. by typing their responses, clicking on an option, or dragging objects into a box).

When some of those features are unfamiliar, cognitive overload may occur not necessarily because of the difficulty of the content being assessed but because those features impose too much information to process. Unusual formats, odd visual arrangements of figures and text, and long or syntactically complex sentences are sources that contribute to an unduly increased cognitive load. In addition to these sources, for ELL students, this cognitive load increase may originate in vocabulary, idiomatic expressions, and contexts (e.g. objects, situations) that are specific to the culture of mainstream students.

Mental Models

Humans have the natural tendency to construct *mental models*—explanations or mental representations of how the world works (Norman, 2013). Ask around why airplanes can fly, why some objects float whereas others sink, or why earthquakes or seasons occur, and the majority of the persons will attempt to offer a theory. Those explanations and representations are created based on both everyday life experiences and knowledge acquired from formal instruction (e.g. what the teacher says or what textbooks show).

Underlying the teaching of any content is a *conceptual model* of a process or phenomenon. This conceptual model allows identification of the elements that are critical to teaching or learning that process or phenomenon. A conceptual model is created purposefully and systematically. In contrast, mental models are continuously evolving in the mind as a result of the interactions an individual has with their environment. Mental models tend to be imprecise, inconsistent, and incomplete. While some may be functional in the sense that they allow individuals to perform certain actions with certain degree of effectiveness, typically they reflect an imprecise understanding of the content.

Norman (1983) has stated that "people's views of the world, of themselves, of their own capabilities, and of the tasks that they are asked to perform, or topics they are asked to learn, depend heavily on the conceptualizations that they bring to the task" (p. 7). This statement makes the relevance of mental models evident to both instruction and assessment. Investigating how students understand a topic paves the way for effective instruction. Also, investigating how students understand what they are supposed to do in completing a task allows interpretations of their responses to tests. This is especially the case for computer-administered tests, in which students need to interact with a computer to obtain and enter information in multiple ways.

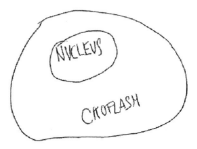

FIGURE 3.1 A student's drawing with a bidimensional representation of a cell.

Students' mental model are inferred from conversations and from activities intended to probe how students think with respect to a given phenomenon or concept. Figure 3.1 shows a Grade 5 student's drawing of a cell. A conversation with the student, when he was asked to explain his drawing, revealed that he thought all cells are flat. The conversation also revealed that this misconception originated from the schematic representations of cells commonly found in science textbooks.

Types of Knowledge

What students know or what a task is intended to assess involves a wide variety of cognitive processes—from simply remembering facts and pieces of information to solving problems and innovating. Several classifications of learning and forms of knowledge have been proposed. Bloom's taxonomy is probably the best-known effort (Anderson *et al.*, 2001; Bloom, 1956; Bloom, Engelhart, Furst, Hill, & Krathwohl, 1956).

The notion that learning takes place according to a specific sequence or hierarchy is not accepted by all authors. Ritchhart, Church, and Morrison (2011) argue that an important limitation of Bloom's taxonomy is its failure to take into consideration context and purpose, which shape the actual sequence in which learning develops. For example, in Anderson and Krathwohl's (2001) taxonomy, understanding is viewed as the second stage in a sequence ranging from lower- to higher-order skills. Yet understanding can vary tremendously in depth and complexity; in many cases it may be a reflection of higher-order skills and expertise.

More recent approaches to addressing different forms of knowledge in assessment (e.g. Ruiz-Primo, 2007; Webb, 2007) are based on the assumption that different levels of academic achievement are linked to different types of knowledge (Ruiz-Primo, 2007). This relationship between level of academic achievement and type of knowledge helps professionals to characterize the form of achievement measured by tests, interpret student test scores, and design or select assessment instruments (Table 3.1).

TABLE 3.1 Framework for Conceptualizing Academic Achievement: Cognitive Dimension. Based on Ruiz-Primo (2007).

Declarative Knowledge (*Knowing That*):
Knowledge of information. From discrete, isolated content elements (e.g. terminology, facts) to organized knowledge (e.g. statements, definitions, classifications, categories, principles, theories).

Procedural Knowledge (*Knowing How*):
Application of procedures, techniques, and methods, usually involving production rules or sequences of steps. From applying algorithms (e.g. adding two numbers) to complex and multi-step procedures (e.g. finding out the density of an object).

Schematic Knowledge (*Knowing Why*):
Knowledge of schemas, mental models, or implicit or explicit "theories" for organizing information in ways that make it possible to apply principles or models to provide explanations and make predictions.

Strategic Knowledge (*Knowing When, Where, and How to Apply Knowledge*):
Domain-specific strategies (e.g. representations of problems or problem solving strategies). Performance monitoring, planning strategies (e.g. dividing a task into subtasks, integrating declarative, procedural, and schematic knowledge).

An important trend in assessment development is the use of learning progressions, which can be thought of as building blocks based on which knowledge can be developed incrementally and coherently, or as roadmaps of learning from novice performance to expert performance (Heritage, 2008; Popham, 2007). Learning progressions can support assessment systems in developing items systematically in ways that all aspects of knowledge relevant to a given content are properly represented in a test (Wilson & Berenthal, 2006). Also, they can be used to create items whose formats and features are determined by the cognitive model according to which students develop the target knowledge or skills (e.g. Briggs, Alonzo, Schwab, & Wilson, 2006).

Used judiciously, taxonomies and progressions provide a conceptual foundation for educators to think critically about the ways in which knowledge is organized. Identifying different types of knowledge allows teachers to develop or select tasks that they can use in support of their teaching. It also allows them to think about the cognitive demands of tasks they give to their students and to judge, for example, how effective and challenging they are as tools for promoting learning.

Whereas all types of knowledge are important, higher-order knowledge and skills are more difficult to teach and assess. Unfortunately, this may lead to overemphasizing basic forms of knowledge over higher-order forms of knowledge. A mistake in teaching and assessing ELL students may consist of not giving them the same kinds of tasks as those given to their non-ELL peers, based on the wrong assumption that limited English proficiency limits their cognitive abilities. This mistake limits ELL students' opportunities to learn.

Expertise

Research on how individuals who are experts in different fields and jobs process information and solve problems has allowed identification of the common characteristics that define an expert (Chi, 2006). This research also has allowed examination of the process of becoming an expert and the characteristics of individuals who are novice and those of individuals who are at intermediate stages in the process of becoming experts. It is known that individuals become experts after being exposed to multiple problems and situations of the same kind.

Characteristics that define an expert include the following:

- use of effective mental strategies for storing and retrieving information;
- ability to identify and use a wide variety of sources of information available to solve a problem;
- automaticity in actions and decision making;
- ability to recognize patterns in the features of multiple problems and situations;
- ability to tell irrelevant features from features that are critical to solving a problem;
- ability to identify problems or situations that are typical of a domain and select the appropriate problem solution strategies;
- tendency to spend as much time as it is necessary to understand the nature of problems and developing representations of those problems; and
- accurate self-monitoring, detecting limitations in their own comprehension of problems.

These characteristics speak to the complexity of cognitive processes and give an accurate idea of what being skilled and knowing a subject in depth actually means. For example, holistic scoring rubrics for the assessment of content knowledge can be created in which the descriptions of performance levels parallel the descriptions of different levels of expertise given by some authors. A consistent finding in the field of expertise is that expert knowledge is developed through practice and experience in an area of specialization (Ericsson & Charness, 1997)—good news, given the common misconception that the characteristics of experts are innate abilities.

Knowing the characteristics of experts also allows examination of assessment tasks and activities. For example, since one of the characteristics of experts is the ability to use multiple sources of information to solve a problem, cognitively challenging tasks can be created for which the solutions take making connections between the information provided by the tasks, and knowledge from different topics previously taught separately. Or, since one of the characteristics of experts is the ability to tell irrelevant features from features that are critical to solving a problem, then the cognitive demands of a hands-on task in which students need to use different pieces of equipment to conduct an experiment can be increased

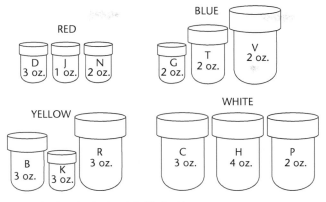

1. Place the bottles in the sink filled with water.
2. Create a chart showing which bottles float and which bottles sink.
3. Based on your observations, what makes object float or sink?
4. Would your results be different if the tub had oil, instead of water? Justify your answer.

FIGURE 3.2 Sink and Float assessment (Grade 4). Students place bottles of different sizes, weights, and colors into a sink filled with water. The color of the bottles, a variable irrelevant to the flotation, adds complexity to the task. Based on Solano-Flores & Shavelson (1997).

by providing pieces of equipment that are relevant and pieces of equipment that are not relevant to successfully conducting the experiment (Figure 3.2).

Metacognitive and Metalinguistic Skills

Metacognition is a term used to refer to the awareness of an individual about their own cognitive processes. These processes concern, among others, learning, memory, and problem solving and involve effectively using previously acquired knowledge (see Schoenfeld, 2004). *Metalinguistic skills* are the skills that enable an individual to think about language and language processes. These processes involve the individuals' own language processes and the processes that are relevant to communicating with other persons through language (Bialystok, 2001).

Both metacognitive and metalinguistic skills have an important value in self-regulation. These skills enable persons to be aware of their own limitations and strengths, to identify the set of demands and affordances of a given situation, to adjust their behavior according to that situation, and to take actions and develop strategies that are adaptive. For example, in reading a challenging passage, a girl with strong metacognitive skills is able to identify when she does not understand a sentence and to parse it out in a way that allows her to find the word, phrase, or grammatical construction that she is having difficulty understanding. Or, in writing in his second language, a boy who is writing a report of an experiment conducted in the science class is aware that discursive styles vary across genres and tries to emulate the style used in science textbooks.

Cognition and Culture

Culture can be defined as the sets of experiences, values, communication styles, forms of socialization, and social practices shared by the members of a social group. *Culture* is a term that sometimes evokes images of ancient or exotic societies or societies that are not the society to which one belongs. In actuality, everybody belongs to cultural groups and all social groups have a culture. Even social groups within a larger social group develop their own cultures, as may be the case of "the culture in a school" or "the culture of the classroom."

Current thinking from the field of sociocultural theory holds that mind (how a person thinks, makes sense of the world, and constructs knowledge) is shaped by culture (Rogoff, 1995; Wertsch, 1985). According to this view, culture influences the ways in which individuals make sense of experience and construct and share knowledge. Three aspects of this influence are particularly relevant to the assessment of ELL students: the ways in which students from different cultural backgrounds learn and share knowledge; the beliefs that students from different cultural backgrounds have about knowledge; and the ways in which negative stereotypes about the knowledge and abilities of the cultural, linguistic, or racial group to which students belong may affect the ways in which they demonstrate knowledge.

Cognitive Cultural Differences

Experience and knowledge are not processed, represented, learned, and shared in the same ways by different cultures. An example of these differences is provided by evidence that individuals from Western and East Asian cultures tend to engage in different perceptual processes involving object and background in images. Whereas individuals from Western cultures tend to focus on the object, independently of the context in which it is embedded, individuals from East Asian cultures tend to use an analytical approach that pays considerable attention to the relationships between the object and the background (Nisbett & Miyamoto, 2005).

An example of cultural differences related to sharing knowledge concerns communication styles. In some cultural groups, giving or offering information on one's thoughts and life only makes sense when the interlocutor also shares information on their thoughts and personal life in the context of a meaningful conversation (Greenfield, 1997). This way of sharing knowledge contrasts with the format of tests in which, typically, items are decontextualized and unrelated to each other. Furthermore, some cultures discourage their children from talking about themselves and their own virtues and accomplishments, which may be considered to be impolite, especially when they talk to adults (Heath, 1983). This form of socialization is in contrast with certain open-ended items which ask students to write about what they know on given topic.

Properly considering cultural differences in cognition is of utmost importance to fair and valid assessment. The information produced by an item is meaningful to the extent to which students' performance on that item is determined by the construct the item is intended to measure, not by cultural influences. Being aware that culture shapes how students interpret and respond to items helps educators to properly interpret the performance of their students. Take as an example the item shown in Figure 3.3. In some cultures, the geometric shape of a square is viewed (and taught) as a category subordinated to the category of rectangles (a square is a special case of rectangle), whereas in other cultures, squares and rectangles are viewed as coordinate categories (Note 3.1). Failing to classify geometric shapes according to the system of categories established by the mathematics curriculum is not necessarily a reflection of inability to learn. In some cases, it may be a reflection of the fact that a student is in the process of appropriating classification conventions used by another culture.

Being aware that culture shapes how students interpret and respond to items also helps educators to examine how the contextual information provided by items with the intent to pose meaningful problems are based on implicit assumptions about the students' cultural experiences or the situations with which they are familiar. As an example, the item shown in Figure 3.4 (US Department of Education, 1999) is not only about rounding and calculating a percentage. The way in which the problem is framed with the intent to provide a meaningful context assumes certain cultural experiences (spending nearly $30 in a restaurant, adding tip of 15 percent). It could be argued that low-income students' performance on this item might be adversely impacted by excessive cognitive load that results from processing contextual information that is unfamiliar.

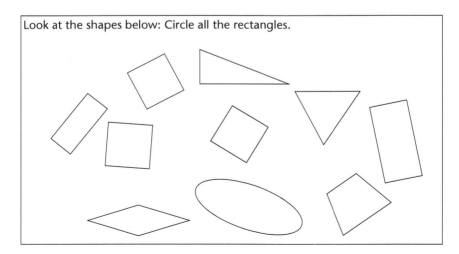

FIGURE 3.3 A hypothetical item intended to assess the ability to recognize geometric figures.

Of the following, which is the closest approximation of a 15 percent tip on a restaurant check of \$24.99?
A.   \$2.50
B.   \$3.00
C.   \$3.75
D.   \$4.50
E.   \$6.00

FIGURE 3.4 Find Amount of Restaurant Tip item. The formatting has been slightly modified. Source: U.S. Department of Education. Office of Educational Research and Improvement. National Center for Education Statistics (1999). *Student Work and Teacher Practices in Mathematics,* NCES 1999–453, by J.H. Mitchell, E.F. Hawkins, P. Jakwerth, F.B. Stancavage, & J.A. Dossey. Washington, DC: Author (p. 64).

Of course, not being familiar with something is not the same as not being able to understand it. Discarding the item on the grounds that cultural differences have an adverse effect on the performance of certain groups might need to be supported by empirical evidence. It is practically impossible to probe how students with different cultural backgrounds reason about each of the items on a test. Yet there is evidence that speaks to the need for scrutinizing items from a perspective that examines culture. First, as mentioned before, students may use knowledge from their personal experience to reason about problems posed by tests (Solano-Flores & Li, 2009). Second, students from different cultural groups may differ on the level of attention they pay to the contextual information provided by items (Solano-Flores, 2011). Third, poverty may influence how students reason about computation problems that involve money (Solano-Flores & Trumbull, 2008).

Personal Epistemologies

The term *personal epistemology* is used to refer to the conceptions individuals develop about knowledge and knowing (Hofer, 2002). These conceptions shape the ways in which individuals learn, understand the world, and make sense of experience.

Personal epistemologies concerning disciplinary knowledge are powerful influences in the process of learning. For example, there is evidence that some of the beliefs students typically have about the nature of mathematics include (Schoenfeld, 1992):

- Mathematical problems have only one solution.
- Mathematical problems can be solved using only one approach.
- Mathematics has little connection with the real world.
- If you know mathematics, you should be able to solve mathematical problems quickly.

As pointed by King and Kitchener (2002), "students' understandings of the nature, limits, and uncertainty in knowledge affects how they approach the process of learning" (p. 55).

Given the social nature of cognition, it is not a surprise that students from different cultures may develop different personal epistemologies about knowledge in the disciplines. For example, students from different cultures may vary on the extent to which they view science as a set of firmly established truths or as entailing a process of inquiry that involves debate and questioning (Bell & Linn, 2002). Also, students from different cultures may have different beliefs about the innate ability to learn (Qian & Pan, 2002).

These findings have important assessment implications. As an example in the classroom context, how students view teachers may influence the ways in which they interact with them. Students from cultures in which teachers are seen as strong authority figures not to be questioned may be less likely than other students to express disagreement in a debate, during a classroom conversation, or to respond to questions from the teacher that require expressing opinions that they feel may be perceived as dissenting.

As an example in the context of large-scale assessment, as part of their approaches to making sense of items, students may focus on different features of items. Students from different cultures may differ on the extent to which they focus on either the content or the contextual information of items and on either the general or specific features of the items (Solano-Flores, 2011).

Stereotype Threat

Stereotype threat is an issue related to bias in testing. It does not concern the characteristics of tests but rather the conditions in which students are tested:

> When a negative stereotype about a group that one is part of becomes personally relevant, usually as an interpretation of one's behavior or an experience one is having, stereotype threat is the resulting sense that one can then be judged or treated in terms of the stereotype or that one might do something that would inadvertently confirm it. (Steele, Spencer, & Aronson, 2002, p. 389)

There is evidence that the ways in which instructions are provided in a testing situation may reflect a cultural stereotype and that the discomfort produced by this threat is strong enough to negatively affect student performance.

The notion of stereotype threat originated from experimental research with college African American students. After controlling for differences between white and African American students (e.g. by ensuring that the samples of participants were equivalent in terms of academic achievement), it was observed that the performance of African American students on tests was lower than the performance of white students when they were reminded that African American students tend to score lower than white students in standardized tests (e.g. "this is a diagnostic test of cognitive ability"). No significant performance differences were observed between white students and African American students who were not reminded about the differences.

Evidence of stereotype threat and its effect on student performance on tests has been found for other minorities and for women (e.g. Aronson, Quinn, & Spencer, 1998; Sherman *et al.*, 2013). Thus, it is not unreasonable to conceive stereotype threat as a factor that affects the performance of ELL students in tests, especially because these students are commonly afflicted by the social stigma associated to their first languages (Valdés, Fishman, Chávez, & Pérez, 2006).

Importantly, the potential for stereotype threat should not be regarded as exclusive of standardized tests. It is also relevant to the classroom context. Everyday assessment activities which exclude ELL students or which imply a view of these students as disabled or dysfunctional (rather than in the process of developing a second language) may potentially contribute to cultural stereotype (see Lee, Deaktor, Enders, & Lambert, 2008). The good news is that educators can take concrete actions to reduce stereotype threat in support of academic performance. These actions include instilling among students the idea that intelligence is a skill that can be strengthened, emphasizing that experiencing difficulties is a natural part of the learning process, and supporting students to not lose sight of the values beyond their experience at school and which makes them worthy (Aronson *et al.*, 2009).

Assessment Activities with Focus on Cognition

Since cognition is not observable, it has to be inferred based on what an individual does or says. Researchers have developed a wide variety of procedures to probe understanding of processes, examine problem solving strategies and mental representations of knowledge, and identify misconceptions (e.g. Ericsson & Simon, 1993; White & Gunstone, 1992). Based on this research, several procedures have been created to examine the cognitive activity underlying student performance on different types of tests (e.g. Baxter, Elder, & Glaser, 1996; Frederikson, Mislevy, & Bejar, 1993; Hamilton, Nussbaum, & Snow, 1997; Ruiz-Primo, Shavelson, Li, & Schultz, 2001). Unfortunately, only some of this work has included ELL students (Winter, Kopriva, Chen, & Emick, 2006).

The principles and procedures generated from that research can be translated into assessment practices focused on understanding the cognitive processes underlying the learning of both ELL and non-ELL students. For example, after giving a quiz with multiple-choice items, a teacher notices that a disproportionately high number of students selected option B—an incorrect option—in one of the items. Beyond simply concluding that many students responded to that item incorrectly, the teacher asks some of them to justify why they chose option B and the reasons why they did not chose the correct option. From the students' explanations, the teacher gains knowledge on both what students know and do not know and how his teaching can be adjusted.

Understanding the reasoning that leads to flawed performance is as important as (or even more important than) understanding the reasoning that leads to successful performance. Having students share their ideas and thinking necessitates a safe classroom environment in which their views are not judged. For teachers unfamiliar with these approaches, it may take some time and practice to resist the impulse of interrupting or correcting students when they share their ideas. It also may take some time and practice for the students of these teachers to get used to the notion that they are not being questioned when they are asked to explain the reasoning underlying an incorrect response.

Thinking Aloud

The term, *think-aloud protocol* (or simply *think-aloud*) is used to refer to an activity in which individuals verbalize the thinking they use in completing a task (e.g. solving a problem, responding to an item). Think-aloud protocols are appropriate in situations in which teachers are interested in understanding the thinking of specific students. They can be concurrent or retrospective. In the former, students are asked to "think aloud" while they complete the task. In the latter, they are asked to report the reasoning they used task after they complete the task.

Students need some training on how to verbalize their thinking the first time they partake in talk aloud protocols. This training is very simple. First, to help them to become familiar with reporting what they think, students are asked a question such as, *Can you tell me how many light bulbs are there in your house?* Some students who are not talkative and find it a bit odd to externalize their thinking may need to be prompted or reminded to think aloud (e.g. *keep thinking aloud... tell me what you're thinking... remember to say what you are thinking*). Then, the student is asked, "Now, tell me what you thought that allowed you to know how many light bulbs there are in your house." After this training, students are given the task of interest and asked to either think aloud while they engage in completing it or after they complete it.

Concurrent and retrospective think-aloud protocols may render different kinds of results. When it is better to use the former or the latter varies depending on the task. Concurrent think-aloud protocols may produce rich information for tasks whose completion takes several minutes (as is the case for hands-on experiments), or tasks involving the solution of a problem or the application of a procedure. Retrospective think-aloud protocols may be more appropriate for tasks whose completion takes around a minute, as is the case for multiple-choice and short-answer items. When retrospective think-alouds are used, students should be asked to report their thinking immediately after they complete the task, not after some time has passed or after the student has completed other tasks.

Reading Aloud

Read-aloud protocols (or *read-alouds*) are activities in which students read aloud an item and rephrase it in their own words. This individual activity is appropriate for teachers to understand the reasoning of specific students they are interested in supporting or when the wording of an item is suspected of misleading the students.

Certainly, having students read aloud items reveals reading struggles or unnecessary reading demands posed by items. Along with these reading difficulties, the read-alouds can reveal what those difficulties reflect. How students read aloud an item and how they rephrase it indicates how they are likely to interpret it. Take as an example the following sentence from an item intended to assess rounding and addition skills (NAEP, 1996):

> His mother has only one-dollar bills.

In an investigation on the ways in which students from different cultural groups interpreted the item (Solano-Flores & Trumbull, 2003), students living in poverty were more likely than other students to read the sentence as:

> His mother has only one dollar.

It is common practice among teachers to examine and discuss the reading demands of items to judge the adequacy of their wording for students at a certain grade level. This form of review and the students' read-aloud should not be thought of as equivalent. The features of items teachers identify as potential reading challenges for their students are not always the same challenges students face. Some features flagged by teachers as potentially challenging do not actually pose a challenge to their students; others, not identified as challenging, are actually challenging. This mismatch speaks to the complexity of cognitive processes. No matter how well teachers know their own students, they do not share with them the same sets of experiences.

Not understanding a word or term in the ways intended by item writers is all it can take for students to produce erroneous interpretations of items. Also, due to cultural differences, ELL students may not be as familiar as their peers are with idiomatic expressions or with contexts provided by items that are assumed to be familiar to everyone. Also, factors related to pragmatics (ways in which the context of text contributes to making meaning) may mislead the interpretation of items, especially for students who are not skilled readers.

Interviews, Small Groups, and Focus Groups

Interviews can be conducted with students individually with the intent to obtain information on specific issues that are not necessarily reported by students during talk-aloud protocols. As with retrospective verbalizations, interviews should be conducted immediately after students have completed a task.

In one interview format, teachers observe students as they complete a task or examine the outcomes of the task (e.g. the response to an item). Then they ask students to justify their actions or their responses, or ask them questions about specific aspects of their performance (e.g. *Why do you say in your answer that the number cannot be divided by two...? I saw you spending a good amount of time seeing the chart with the numbers. Why was that?*)

In another interview format, teachers ask students questions they have prepared in advance with the purpose of learning how they make sense of the items. Examples of these questions include:

- Is there anything that you found confusing in this problem?
- What are words or phrases that you don't know or find confusing in this item?
- How would you explain in your own words this problem to a friend?

Students' responses to these questions allow identification of both ways in which tasks can be improved and ways in which their experiences influence how students interpret items.

Having students work in teams on constructed-response tasks that require providing justifications and explanations promotes rich conversation that reflects how they think. This activity can be used in combination with focus groups. The teacher assembles a small group of students. After they complete a task, the teacher facilitates a discussion to obtain information on their thinking and the problem solving strategies they used. The discussion can be guided by questions like the ones shown above.

Interviews and small and focus groups do not necessarily produce the same information. Focus groups should be used when the goal is to have a sense of the thinking and reasoning used by students when they take tests, without focusing on particular students. They promote rich discussions in which the participation of a student promotes the participation of other students.

Multimodal Representations of Knowledge

Additional methods for probing understanding and investigating students' mental models involve the use of multiple *semiotic modalities* (forms of representation of information). One method consists of giving students a list of concepts on a given topic and representing the topic with drawings in which concepts are shown as nodes (circles), and the relations between those concepts are shown with arrows and short statements describing those relations (Figure 3.5). Another method consists of asking students to represent in writing and with drawings how they think about a given phenomenon or concept (Figure 3.6).

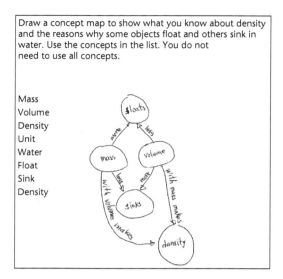

Draw a concept map to show what you know about density and the reasons why some objects float and others sink in water. Use the concepts in the list. You do not need to use all concepts.

Mass
Volume
Density
Unit
Water
Float
Sink
Density

FIGURE 3.5 A concept map task intended to probe understanding of the concept of relative density, and a student's response.

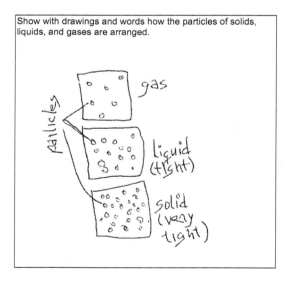

Show with drawings and words how the particles of solids, liquids, and gases are arranged.

FIGURE 3.6 A task intended to probe understanding of basic ideas on the structure of matter. Adapted from Scott, P. H. (1992). Pathways in learning science: A case study of the development of one student's ideas relating to the structure of matter. In R. Duit, F. Goldber, and H. Niedderer (Eds.), *Research in physics learning: Theoretical issues and empirical studies: Proceedings of an international workshop.* Kiel, Germany: Institut für die Pädogogik der Naturwissenschaften an der Universität Kiel (pp. 203–224).

Supported by conversations in which students explain and discuss their representations, these activities may be especially engaging for ELL students, as they expand the variety of resources they can use to present and discuss their ideas.

Closing Comments

Assessment is more effective when it is focused on the cognitive processes underlying learning. The need for addressing cognition from a cultural perspective arises from the fact that tests, assessment activities, and assessment systems are cultural products. As with any cultural product, they reflect the characteristics of the predominant culture of the society in which they originate. How effectively students make sense of items and respond to them is shaped by the level of familiarity they have with the experiences, values, communication styles, and forms of socialization of the society in which tests are created.

Taking into consideration how culture shapes the ways in which students interpret test items and respond to them enables educators to make proper interpretations of their students' performance and to be aware of the multiple ways in which tests are constructed based on (correct or flawed) assumptions about the students' familiarity with everyday life situations commonly used in tests to contextualize problems.

As part of their teaching and assessment practices, educators can use multiple procedures generated from educational research and research on cognition. Information obtained from students' talk-alouds and read-alouds, and from conducting focus groups, interviews, and activities intended to probe understanding can help educators to develop a sense of the learning styles of their students, how they understand the concepts being taught, how they understand items, and how they relate their experience to the content being taught and to the content of test items. This information is also helpful to understand how first language influences, differences in communication styles, and the fact that ELL students are still developing English as a second language, shape how these students learn and interpret test items.

Exercises

Exercise 3.1: Mental Models

1. Ask your students to explain in writing and with drawings why, on a hot summer day, when you pour cold water in a glass, water drops form on its surface.
(Note: You do not need to be a science teacher to be able to perform this activity. The answer to the question is that the water vapor in the air around the glass condensates on the cold surface of the glass.)
2. Examine your students' work and make an attempt to infer how your students think about condensation. Do not simply focus on whether the responses are

correct or incorrect. Let the students give their explanations so that you can learn how they think.

3. Have conversations with some of your ELL students and ask them to explain in more detail what they drew and wrote.

4. What can you conclude about the ways in which students think about condensation?

5. How can you incorporate the knowledge gained from this experience into your teaching practices, especially with ELL students?

Exercise 3.2: Types of Knowledge and Cognitive Processes

1. Respond to the items shown in Figure 3.7. It does not matter if you are not sure about some of your responses. Pay attention to the reasoning and knowledge you have to use to solve the problems.

2. Figure 3.8 shows a summary of Anderson and Krathwohl's framework for learning, teaching, and assessing. Examine carefully the definitions of each type of knowledge and each cognitive process. (Note 3.2)

3. Using the format shown in Figure 3.8, identify the combination of type of knowledge and cognitive process involved in the solution of each of the division problems you solved above.

4. Write the number of each item in the appropriate cell, to identify where in the chart each of the division problems above goes.

Item 1.
$2,375 / 49 = \square$

Item 2.
Is $956 \times .3$ a division?   Yes____ No____
Justify your answer.

Item 3.
John serves 16 liters of lemonade in 6-oz. cups. How many cups can he fill with lemonade?

Item 4.
In the division, $Q = R / S$, Q will be >1 if

A) $S < R$, $R \neq 0$, and $S \neq 0$
B) $S > R$, $R \neq 0$, and $S \neq 0$
C) $S = Q$, $R \neq 0$, and $S \neq 0$

FIGURE 3.7 Mathematics items.

FIGURE 3.8 Format for examining test items according to type of knowledge and cognitive process. Based on Anderson *et al.* (2001).

Cognitive Process	Type of Knowledge			
	Factual: Basic elements of knowledge in a discipline (vocabulary, facts).	**Conceptual:** Interrelationships among elements within a topic.	**Procedural:** Ways of doing things; methods, procedures, techniques, algorithms, etc.	**Meta-cognitive:** Awareness of cognition and the complexity of knowledge.
Remember: Retrieve knowledge from memory.	1,1	1,2	1,3	1,4
Understand: Make sense of information represented in multiple forms.	2,1	2,2	2,3	2,4
Apply: Use knowledge in a familiar or new situation.	3,1	3,2	3,3	3,4
Analyze: Divide material (e.g. content, information) into its components and identify how they are related.	4,1	4,2	4,3	4,4
Evaluate: Judge the appropriateness or consistency of processes, procedures, methods, etc.	5.1	5.2	5.3	5.4
Create: Assemble elements (e.g. ideas, pieces of information) and organizing or reorganizing them coherently.	6.1	6.2	6.3	6.4

5. Create one item of the content of your choice for each the following cells in the chart:
   (1,4)
   (2,2)
   (3,4)
   (4,2)
6. Think about a specific lesson or topic you like to teach. In which cells in the chart would you place the exercises and assessment activities you typically use with your students to assess their learning?
7. How can you use the chart to reflect on your teaching and assessment practices and ensure that the exercises and assessment activities that you use with your students (including ELL students) cover a wide variety of cells?

Exercise 3.3: Examining Cultural Influences in Students' Interpretations of Items

1. Give the following (NAEP, 1996) item to two ELL and two non-ELL students. Ask them to show their work and reasoning with numbers, words, and drawings.

Sam can purchase his lunch at school. Each day he wants to have juice that costs 50¢, a sandwich that cost 90¢, and fruit that costs 35¢. His mother has only $1.00 bills. What is the least number of $1.00 bills that his mother should give him so he will have enough money to buy lunch for five days?

---

2. Once the students respond to the item, have a short individual interview with each of them. Ask them the following questions:
   - How do you see what happens in Sam's story as part of what you do when you are at school?
   - How do you see what happens in Sam's story as part of what you do for fun when you are not at school?
3. What commonalities and differences can you identify in the ways in which your students relate the content of the item with their own lives? Can any difference influence the ways in which they understand the item and respond to it? Do different levels of proficiency in English or different sets of cultural experiences influence the ways in which your ELL students understand the item? How?

Exercise 3.4: Examining Students' Item Views

1. Select an item that is appropriate to the grade and content you teach. Make sure that the item is complex, involves the solution of a problem, and uses contextual information (e.g. fictitious characters, a story) with the intent to make the problem meaningful.
2. Give the item to two ELL and two non-ELL students. Ask them to show their work and reasoning with numbers, words, and drawings.
3. After they respond to the item, have a short interview with each of the students selected. Ask them the following questions:
    *   What is this item about?
    *   What do you think you need to know to be able to respond to it correctly?
4. Based on the students' responses to the first question, do you think the students focus overly on the context (the story) of the item and not much on the content (the problem) of the item? If so, does that have an effect on whether they respond to the item correctly?
5. Based on the students' responses to the second question, do you think they are able to identify the content (e.g. topic, type of knowledge) the item is intended to assess? How might the ability to identify the content of items affect their ability to respond correctly to them?
6. Are there any differences between ELL and non-ELL students' responses? How do proficiency in English and different sets of cultural experiences account for those differences? How can you use the knowledge gained from this experience to inform the way in which you teach and assess your students?

Notes

Note 3.1. Surprisingly, even within the same society, definitions and conceptualizations of quadrilaterals vary over time and across curricula, as Usiskin & Dougherty (2007) have shown.

Note 3.2. These definitions have been simplified for the purpose of this exercise. For a detailed discussion, see the original source (Anderson *et al.*, 2001).

References

Anderson, L. W., Krathwohl, D. R. (Eds.), Airasian, P. W., Cruikshank, K. A., Mayer, R. E., Pintrich, P. R., Raths, J., & Wittrock, M. C. (2001). *A taxonomy for learning, teaching, and assessing: A revision of Bloom's Taxonomy of Educational Objectives* (Complete edition). New York: Longman.

Aronson, J., Cohen, G., McColskey, W., Montrosse, B., Lewis, K., and Mooney, K. (2009). *Reducing stereotype threat in classrooms: a review of social-psychological intervention studies on improving the achievement of Black students* (Issues & Answers Report, REL 2009–No. 076). Washington, DC: US Department of Education, Institute of Education Sciences, National Center for Education Evaluation and Regional Assistance, Regional Educational Laboratory Southeast. Retrieved July 31, 2015 from http://ies.ed.gov/ncee/edlabs.

Aronson, J., Quinn, D. M., & Spencer, S. J. (1998). Stereotype threat and the academic performance of women and minorities. In J. K. Swim & C. Stangor (Eds.), *Prejudice: The target's perspective* (pp. 83–103). San Diego: Academic Press.

Baxter, G. P., Elder, A. D., & Glaser, R. (1996). Knowledge-based cognition and performance assessment in the science classroom. *Educational Psychologist, 31*(2), 133–140.

Bell, P., & Linn, M. C. (2002). Beliefs about science: How does science instruction contribute? In B. K. Hofer & P. R. Pintrich (Eds.), *Personal epistemology: The psychology of beliefs about knowledge and knowing* (pp. 321–346). Mahwah, NJ: Lawrence Erlbaum Associates, Publishers.

Bialystok, E. (2001). *Bilingualism in development: Language, literacy, and cognition.* Cambridge, UK: Cambridge University Press.

Bloom, B. S. (1956). *Taxonomy of educational objectives: The classification of educational goals. Handbook 1: Cognitive domain.* New York: David McKay Company, Inc.

Bloom, B. S., Engelhart, M. D., Furst, E. J., Hill, W. H., & Krathwohl, D. R. (Eds.) (1956). *Taxonomy of educational objectives: The classification of educational goals: Handbook 1: Cognitive domain.* London, WI: Longmans, Green & Co. Ltd.

Briggs, D. C., Alonzo, A. C., Schwab, C., & Wilson, M. (2006). Diagnostic assessment with ordered multiple-choice items. *Educational Assessment, 11*(1), 33–63.

Chi, M. T. H. (2006). Two approaches to the study of experts' characteristics. In K. A. Ericsson, N. Charness, P. J. Feltovich, & R. R. Hoffman (Eds.), *The Cambridge handbook of expertise and expert performance.* Cambridge, NY: Cambridge University Press.

Ericsson, K. A. & Charness, N. (1997). Cognitive and developmental factors in expert performance. In P. J. Feltovich, K. M. Ford, & R. R. Hoffman (Eds.), *Expertise in context: Human and machine.* Menlo Park, CA: AAAI Press/The MIT Press.

Ericsson, K. A. & Simon, H. S. (1993). *Protocol analysis: Verbal reports as data.* Cambridge, MA: The MIT Press.

Frederikson, N., Mislevy, R. J., & Bejar, I. I. (1993). *Test theory for a new generation of tests.* Hillsdale, NJ: Lawrence Erlbaum Associates.

Greenfield, P. M. (1997). Culture as process: Empirical methods for cultural psychology. In J. W. Berry, Y. H. Poortinga, & J. Pandey (Eds.), *Handbook of cross-cultural psychology, Second Edition. Vol. 1: Theory and method* (pp. 301–346). Needham Heights, MA: Allyn & Bacon.

Hamilton, L. S., Nussbaum, E. M., & Snow, R. E. (1997). Interview procedures for validating science assessments. *Applied Measurement in Education, 10,* 181–200.

Hamilton, L. S., Nussbaum, E. M., Kupermintz, H., Kerkhoven, J. I. M., & Snow, R. S. (1997). Enhancing the validity and usefulness of large-scale educational assessments: II. NELS:88 Science Achievement. *American Educational Research Journal, 32*(3), 555–581.

Heath, S. B. (1983). *Ways with words: Language, life and work in communities and classrooms.* Cambridge, UK: Cambridge University Press.

Heritage, M. (February, 2008). *Learning progressions: Supporting instruction and formative assessment.* Washington, DC: Council of Chief State School Officers.

Hofer, B. K. (2002). Personal epistemology as a psychological and educational construct: An introduction. In B. K. Hofer & P. R. Pintrich (Eds.), *Personal epistemology: The psychology of beliefs about knowledge and knowing* (pp. 3–14). Mahwah, NJ: Lawrence Erlbaum Associates, Publishers.

King, P. M. & Kitchener, K. S. (2002). The reflective judgment model: Twenty years of research on epistemic cognition. In B. K. Hofer & P. R. Pintrich (Eds.), *Personal epistemology: The psychology of beliefs about knowledge and knowing* (pp. 37–61). Mahwah, NJ: Lawrence Erlbaum Associates, Publishers.

Lee, O., Deaktor, R., Enders, C., & Lambert, J. (2008). Impact of a multiyear professional development intervention on science achievement of culturally and linguistically diverse students. *Journal of Research in Science Teaching, 45*(6), 726–747.

National Assessment of Educational Progress (1996). *Mathematics items public release.* Washington, DC: Author.

Nisbett, R. E. & Miyamoto, Y. (2005). The influence of culture: holistic versus analytic perception. *TRENDS in Cognitive Sciences, 9*(10). 467–473.

Norman, D. (1983). Introduction. In D. Gentner & A. L. Stevens (Eds.), *Mental models.* Hillsdale, NJ: Lawrence Erlbaum Associates, Publishers.

Norman, D. (2013). *The design of everyday things: Revised and expanded edition.* New York: Basic Books.

Office of Educational Research and Improvement. National Center for Education Statistics (1999). *Student Work and Teacher Practices in Mathematics,* NCES 1999–453, by J. H. Mitchell, E. F. Hawkins, P. Jakwerth, F. B. Stancavage, & J. A. Dossey. Washington, DC: Author.

Popham, J. W. (April 2007). The lowdown on learning progressions. *Educational Leadership, 64*(7), 83–84.

Qian, G. & Pan, J. (2002). A comparison of epistemological beliefs and learning from science text between American and Chinese high school students. In B. K. Hofer & P. R. Pintrich (Eds.), *Personal epistemology: The psychology of beliefs about knowledge and knowing* (pp. 365–385). Mahwah, NJ: Lawrence Erlbaum Associates, Publishers.

Rogoff, B. (1995). Observing sociocultural activity on three planes: participatory appropriation, guided participation, and apprenticeship. In J. V. Wertsch, P. del Río, & A. Alvarez (Eds.), *Sociocultural studies of mind*. New York: Cambridge University Press.

Ruiz-Primo, M. A. (2007). Assessment in science and mathematics: Lessons learned. In M. Hoepfl & M. Lindstrom (Eds.), *Assessment of Technology Education, CTTE 56th Yearbook* (pp. 203–232). Woodland Hills, CA: Glencoe-McGraw Hill.

Ruiz-Primo, M. A., Shavelson, R. J., Li, M., & Schutlz, S. E. (2001). On the validity of cognitive interpretations of scores from alternative mapping techniques. *Educational Assessment, 7*(2), 99–141.

Schoenfeld, A. H. (1992). Learning to think mathematically: Problem solving, metacognition, and sense-making in mathematics. In D. Grouws (Ed.), *Handbook for research on mathematics teaching and learning* (pp. 334–370). New York: MacMillan.

Schoenfeld, A. H. (2004). The math wars. *Educational Policy, 18*(1), 253–286.

Scott, P. H. (1992). Pathways in learning science: A case study of the development of one student's ideas relating to the structure of matter. In R. Duit, F. Goldberg, & H. Niedderer (Eds.), *Research in physics learning: Theoretical issues and empirical studies: Proceedings of an international workshop* (pp. 203–224). Kiel, Germany: Institut für die Pädogogik der Naturwissenschaften an der Universität Kiel.

Sherman, D. K., Hartson, K, A., Binning, K. R., Purdie-Vaughns, V., Garcia, J., Taborsky-Barba, S., Tomassetti, S., Nussbaum, A. D., & Cohen, G. L. (2013). Deflecting the trajectory and changing the narrative: How self-affirmation affects academic performance and motivation under identity threat. *Journal of Personality and Social Psychology, 104*(4), 591–618.

Solano-Flores, G. (2011). Assessing the cultural validity of assessment practices: An introduction. In M. R. Basterra, E. Trumbull, & G. Solano-Flores (Eds.), *Cultural validity in assessment: Addressing linguistic and cultural diversity* (pp. 3–21). New York: Routledge.

Solano-Flores, G. & Li, M. (2009). Generalizability of cognitive interview-based measures across cultural groups. *Educational Measurement: Issues and Practice, 28*(2), 9–18.

Solano-Flores, G. & Trumbull, E. (2003). Examining language in context: The need for new research and practice paradigms in the testing of English-language learners. *Educational Researcher, 32*(2), 3–13.

Solano-Flores, G. & Trumbull, E. (2008). In what language should English language learners be tested? In R. J. Kopriva (Ed.), *Improving testing for English language learners: A comprehensive approach to designing, building, implementing and interpreting better academic assessments* (pp. 169–200). New York: Routledge.

Solano-Flores, G., Shade, C., & Chrzanowski, A. (2014). *Item accessibility and language variation conceptual framework. Submitted to the Smarter Balanced Assessment Consortium.* October 10. http://www.smarterbalanced.org/wordpress/wp-content/uploads/2014/11/ItemAccessibilityandLanguageVariation ConceptualFramework_11-10.pdf.

Steele, C. M., Spencer, S. J., & Aronson, J. (2002). Contending with group image: The psychology of stereotype and social identity threat. *Advances in Experimental Social Psychology, 34,* 379–440.

Sweller, J. (1994). Cognitive load theory, learning difficulty, and instructional design. *Learning and Instruction, 4,* 295–312.

US Department of Education. Office of Educational Research and Improvement. National Center for Education Statistics (1999). *Student Work and Teacher Practices in Mathematics,* NCES 1999–453, by J. H. Mitchell, E. F. Hawkins, P. Jakwerth, F. B. Stancavage, & J. A. Dossey. Washington, DC: Author. Retrieved July 30, 2015 from http://nces.ed.gov/nationsreportcard/pdf/main1996/1999453a.pdf.

Usiskin, Z. & Dougherty, B. J. (2007). *The classification of quadrilaterals: A study in definition.* Charlotte, NC: Information Age Publishing.

Valdés, G., Fishman, J. A., Chavez, R. M, & Perez, W. (Eds.)(2006). *Developing Minority Language Resources: The Case of Spanish in California.* Clevedon, England: Multilingual Matters.

Webb. N. L.(2007). Issues related to judging the alignment of curriculum standards and assessments. *Applied Measurement in Education, 20*(1), 7–25.

Wertsch, J.V. (Ed.)(1985). *Culture, communication and cognition: Vygotskian perspectives.* Cambridge, UK: Cambridge University Press.

White, R. T. & Gunstone, R. F. (1992). *Probing Understanding.* London: Falmer Press.

WIDA (2012). Amplification of the English Language Development Standards: Kindergarten–Grade 12. Wisconsin: Board of Regents of the University of Wisconsin System.

Wilson, M. R. & Berenthal, M. W. (Eds.)(2006). *Systems for state science assessment.* Washington, DC: National Academy Press.

Winter, P., Kopriva, R. J., Chen, S., & Emick, J. (2006). Exploring individual and item factors that affect assessment validity for diverse learners: Results from a large-scale cognitive lab. *Learning and Individual Differences, 16,* 267–276.

4

ASSESSMENT OF LANGUAGE PROFICIENCY

Overview

This chapter addresses the challenges of assessing language proficiency. It discusses the limitations of instruments intended to assess language proficiency and how the information they produce needs to be interpreted judiciously in order to make sound decisions concerning specific students' English proficiency. Mandatory testing of English proficiency may have as an unintended consequence that educators rely exclusively on information from large-scale tests on their own students without proper interpretation or without using that information along with information from other sources. This chapter provides educators with concepts and ideas that are relevant to reasoning about language assessment and to using language proficiency tests critically.

The section "The Challenges of Assessing Proficiency in English as a Second Language" discusses the elusiveness of the concept of language proficiency, the limitations of tests intended to measure English proficiency, and the ways in which inaccurate information about English proficiency may mislead educators in the decisions they make concerning ELL students.

The section "Examining Language Proficiency Assessments" discusses some of the procedures used to develop language proficiency assessments. It contends that, whereas language tests produce valuable information about ELL students' proficiency in English, this information should be used with caution.

The section "Using and Obtaining Information on English Proficiency" offers strategies that educators can use to properly use language assessments and interpret information from these instruments. It also offers strategies educators can use to make content- and context-sensitive judgments about the English proficiency of their ELLs.

The Challenges of Assessing Proficiency in English as a Second Language

What Counts as Being Proficient in a Language

A serious challenge in the assessment of ELL students' proficiency in English is the view of language proficiency as a discrete condition—a person is or is not proficient in a language. In actuality, even in their first, native language, people may have different levels of proficiency. For example, two persons whose first language is English may differ on the vocabulary they use frequently, the ability with which they express their ideas or emotions, the ease or difficulty with which they read text on different topics, or their familiarity with certain idiomatic expressions. These differences may occur even if these two persons have considerable sets of shared experiences and comparable histories and levels of formal education.

A person's level of proficiency in a language is shaped by the context in which language is used (MacSwan, 2000). The two native English users in the example above may not be as effective in communicating their ideas or understanding other people's ideas in English when they need to interact with persons from different origins, professions, or socioeconomic status, and when they read materials or talk about topics with which they are not familiar. The fact that individuals do not cease to learn or encounter new words and expressions is a proof that, strictly speaking, no one is totally proficient in a language. That an individual is or is not proficient in a language should be interpreted as very general statement.

One of the challenges in assessing English proficiency in ELL students stems from the fact that developing a first language and developing a second language are wrongly assumed to be the same process. Serious limitations to the proper use of tests and the proper interpretation of test scores may result from not considering important differences between the two processes. Using the behavior or skills of native users of English as a benchmark for proficiency in English as a second language may lead to emphasizing specific aspects of English proficiency that may not be relevant to developing English as a second language. Thinking about English proficiency among ELL students should take into consideration the commonalities and differences of being functionally fluent in the first and in the second language. For example, to be considered as English proficient, should ELL students be expected to have a pronunciation in English similar to the pronunciation of native English users? Should the words or families of words critical for an ELL to be able to benefit from instruction be determined based on the vocabulary of native English users? Should it be assumed that the social contexts in which English is used are the same for ELLs and native English speakers?

Monolingual and Bilingual Perspectives of Language Proficiency

Bilingual individuals cannot be effectively evaluated based on monolingual views (Hopewell & Escamilla, 2013). The main reason is that bilingual individuals have functional fluency in two languages (Bialystok, 2001). Of course, this fluency is distributed between two languages (see Oller, Pearson, & Cobo-Lewis, 2007). Also, this fluency for each language does not have the same appearance as the fluency for monolingual native users of each language.

Unfortunately, testing policies concerning ELLs are not always sensitive to this notion (Hakuta, 2000). Authors have expressed concerns about testing ELL students with tests of English proficiency originally created to assess native English users. Also, authors have expressed concerns about policies concerning language development that focus on English proficiency among ELLs without taking into consideration proficiency in their native language (e.g. August & Hakuta, 1997; August & Shanahan, 2006).

Table 4.1 illustrates how failure to consider the fact that ELLs are developing two languages leads to drawing incorrect conclusions about their linguistic abilities. The table shows the number of different words two boys (José, an ELL, and Bill, a non-ELL) were able to name (see Escamilla, 2000). If only English is taken into consideration, José's language development is seen as lower than Bill's development.

> José (should) receive credit for knowing six colors (3 in Spanish + 3 in English). However, because the school measures progress in each language separately (as if José were two monolinguals), he is viewed as not being well-developed in either language. (Escamilla, 2000, p. 13)

Consistent with the notion that a bilingual person is not the sum of two monolinguals (Grosjean, 1989; Valdés & Figueroa, 1994), there is evidence that very different conclusions based on the same set of data are drawn about the reading skills of ELL students depending on whether monolingual or bilingual frameworks are used to interpret student performance (Hopewell & Escamilla, 2013).

Not considering the proficiency of ELL students in their first language leads to drawing inaccurate conclusions about their language development and cognitive skills and, in the worst cases, may contribute to erroneous referral decisions to special education programs (Abedi, 2007; MacSwan & Rolstad, 2006). A long-standing concern in the field of special education is that linguistic, racial, and cultural minorities are unduly overrepresented in special education programs

TABLE 4.1 Vocabulary as an Indicator of Language Proficiency: Number of Different Colors Named by Two 5-Year-Old Children in Two Languages. Adapted from Escamilla (2000).

	in English	in Spanish	Total
José	3	3	6
Bill	5	0	5

(Artiles, Trent, & Palmer, 2004). Educators who make ELL student referral decisions to these special education programs do not necessarily act based on knowledge on second language acquisition and may confuse developing English proficiency with cognitive disability. They may attribute poor academic performance to factors intrinsic to the students, without taking into consideration that these students are developing English as a second language (Klingner & Harry, 2006).

Educators can better inform their teaching and serve the needs of their ELL students by becoming critical users of tests of English proficiency and selecting these tests and interpreting the scores they produce judiciously. Also, they can develop a sense of each of their ELL students' English proficiency based on both formal and informal sources of information. Contrary to what common sense might dictate, developing these strategies does not require educators to be speakers of their ELL students' native language.

Examining Language Proficiency Assessments

In selecting instruments intended to assess language development among ELL students, it is important to be mindful about the limitations of measures of English proficiency discussed above. Also, it is important to examine how those instruments have been developed. The process of development of an instrument (or the information provided about that process) reflects the extent to which important principles of language and language development have been taken into consideration.

Assessment Frameworks

An important indicator of the quality of a test of English proficiency is the quality of its assessment framework, a document that offers a conception of the domain of interest and the types of knowledge and skills it comprises, and a discussion of how these types of knowledge and skills are organized. The framework should be supported by current knowledge on language development and bilingual development.

Figure 4.1 shows a possible way of representing the organization of the English proficiency domain. This organization is represented as the intersection of different language modes (listening, reading, speaking, and writing), and different social contexts. Called a *content matrix*, this representation of the domain of knowledge and skills allows systematic generation of items for each cell.

Standards

The development of an instrument must be supported by standards documents—documents that specify what students should know and be able to do at a given

Social Contexts	Language Mode			
	Reception		Production	
	Listening	Reading	Speaking	Writing
Learning in the Classroom				
Interacting with Peers				
Interacting with Adults				
Everyday Life				

FIGURE 4.1 Hypothetical content matrix for developing an English proficiency test.

grade for a given domain of knowledge and skills (see Raizen, 1997). Evidence that an instrument assesses certain knowledge and skills is referred to as the alignment of the instrument with the standards. In judging whether an instrument is appropriate to assess English proficiency among ELL students, it is important to keep in mind that English language arts, English as a first language, English as a foreign language, and English as a second language are different domains. While these domains have commonalities, they differ in important ways concerning the social contexts in which language is used and the characteristics of the target populations.

Of utmost importance is the difference between English as a foreign language and English as a second language (see Gass & Selinker, 2001). A foreign language is *learned* as a subject in the social environment in which the individual's native language is spoken, typically in a formal instructional context (e.g. native English users in the US take classes of Spanish in their schools, in which instruction is in English). In contrast, a second language is *acquired* mainly through social interaction in the environment in which that language is predominant (e.g. native Spanish users living in the US develop English out of necessity from living in a predominantly English speaking society).

Given these important differences, the extent to which a test assesses the kind of English proficiency ELL students need to succeed academically depends on the standards used to create it. Tests created based on English development standards for monolingual individuals are not sensitive to the characteristics of language development in two languages. Likewise, tests created based on English language arts or English as a foreign language standards are likely to emphasize normative and formal aspects of language (e.g. grammatical rules, pronunciation, and spelling) over functional aspects (e.g. communication skills that are necessary to benefit from instruction in English).

The WIDA (World-Class Instructional Design and Assessment) standards (WIDA, 2012) and the English Language Proficiency Development Framework (CCSSO, 2012) are important documents that will potentially contribute to more valid, fair assessment for ELLs. WIDA's framework focuses on academic language, which is "viewed as a vehicle for communicating and learning within sociocultural contexts" and recognizes that the uses of language are influenced by "the interactions between different people for specific purposes and across different learning environments" (WIDA, 2012, p. v). The English Language Proficiency Framework is intended "to provide guidance to states on how to use the expectations of the Common Core State standards and the [Next Generation Science Standards] as tools for the creation and evaluation of ELP standards." (CCSSO, 2012, p. 1)

WIDA's licensed assessments for K–12 students are being used by multiple states with the purpose of determining English proficiency and eligibility for English as a Second Language services and to monitor progress in English development. In addition to WIDA, another state consortium, ELPA21 and three states are developing English language proficiency assessments that emphasize skills relevant to the Common Core State Standards (Hakuta, 2015).

While the effectiveness of all these assessments cannot be judged at this time, they are likely to produce more valuable information on English proficiency than other English proficiency assessments. First, the standards documents based on which these assessments are developed have a theoretical perspective of bilingualism. As a consequence, they are more sensitive to the social context of language and the aspects of communication that are common across content areas (Walqui, 2015). Second, because these assessments' content emphasizes competencies that correspond to the Common Core State Standards, they may provide educators with information on performance that is more meaningful to their practice (Hakuta, 2015).

Test Development Process

Critical to the quality of tests is the process through which they are developed (Solano-Flores, 2011). As part of the process of development, the items need to be tried out several times with samples of students that are representative of the population of students with which the test will be used. Each time the items are tried with these samples of students, information is obtained about the clarity of tasks and whether the items elicit behavior or reasoning that is relevant to the constructs the items are intended to measure.

Information on the numbers and characteristics of the students used in the process of development of a test of English proficiency is critical to judging its quality. As mentioned before, developing proficiency in English as a second language is not the same as developing English as a first language, learning English as a foreign language, or learning English language arts. Accordingly, the samples of pilot students should be composed of students who meet the profile of ELL students, not students of English as a foreign language or students whose native language is English.

Using and Obtaining Information on English Proficiency

Challenges in the Assessment of English Proficiency

The vastness of language as a domain of knowledge and skills poses a limit to the dependability of measures of language proficiency. As discussed in Chapter 1, a test can be thought of as a sample of observations on a knowledge domain. Thus, in order to allow proper generalizations (conclusions) about an individual's proficiency in English as a second language at a given age or grade, the size of the sample (number of items) and the characteristics of the items (their content, the knowledge and skills they elicit) must be representative of the domain.

The multiple patterns of language dominance among ELL students is another factor that contributes to the challenges of assessing English proficiency. Each bilingual individual has a unique set of strengths and weaknesses in their first and in their second language. As a consequence, a category such as "Limited English Proficient" does not convey information about the set of strengths and weaknesses of each student in each language mode that teachers can use to inform their teaching. Even when assessment systems provide detailed information on English proficiency along with scores or performance levels, it cannot be assumed that that information is always made available to teachers in a timely manner, so that they can plan and differentiate their instruction to serve their students' individual needs.

Given these circumstances, it becomes clear that, in order to develop a sense of each of their ELL students' proficiency in English, educators need to interpret test results judiciously and to use multiple sources of information on their students' English proficiency.

Confusion Matrix

Because of the vastness of language as a domain of knowledge and skills, tests of English proficiency may emphasize different aspects of language. For example, some tests may emphasize word recognition over conversational skills or may provide different sets of contexts in which language is used. This is not necessarily a problem, as long as the generalizations made about the students' English proficiency are circumscribed to the specific skills assessed. However, since many of the commercially available tests of English proficiency focus on vocabulary (one among many aspects of English proficiency) (see García, McKoon, & August, 2006), schools or teachers may have a limited set of options regarding the tests they can give to their ELL students. As a consequence, they may end up relying only on those tests to assess their students' proficiency in English.

A *confusion matrix* helps to appreciate the implications of using only one test to make decisions concerning proficiency in English (see Solano-Flores, 2012).

A confusion matrix is a device that facilitates reasoning about the consistency of two given tests in their classifications of students as limited English proficient (LEP). Suppose that Test A and Test B have been created to assess proficiency in English as a second language and that both have comparable technical qualities. Suppose also that these tests are given to the same set of students with the purpose of identifying who should and who should not be considered as limited English proficient. As Figure 4.2 shows, four classification cases exist:

- A student is identified as LEP by both Test A and Test B (Cell h)
- A student is identified as LEP by Test A, not Test B (Cell i)
- A student is identified as LEP by Test B, not Test A (Cell j)
- A student is not identified as LEP by either Test A or Test B (Cell k)

If the two tests render entirely consistent results, all students who take them will be in Cells h and k. Yet it is more realistic to expect some cases in which students will be in Cells i and j. One reason for this inconsistency may be that the two tests are sensitive to different aspects of language proficiency. Measures of English proficiency are not perfect. Ideally, several measures should be used in combination to assess ELL students' English proficiency and those measures should be used judiciously.

It must be said that inconsistent or inaccurate classifications of students are not specific to tests of language proficiency. Indeed, measurement specialists spend a great deal of their time estimating the technical qualities of tests to ensure that the proportions of false positive and false negative classifications tests produce are within an acceptable range.

Linguagrams

Educators make better decisions concerning their ELL students when they are provided with detailed information about these students' proficiency in English (Cheatham, Jimenez-Silva, Wodrich, & Kasai, 2014). Using multiple measures of English proficiency judiciously entails interpreting information from tests in context, based on the teacher's own knowledge of the characteristics of each of their

		Test A	
		Limited English Proficient	English Proficient
Test B	Limited English Proficient	h	i
	English Proficient	j	k

FIGURE 4.2 Confusion matrix for evaluating consistency in the classification of students produced by two tests of English proficiency.

students. Educators may make the mistake of developing perceptions about their ELL students' proficiency in English based on information from only one test or from tests that do not produce detailed information on English proficiency, or based on outdated information on the proficiency of those students. This mistake may occur especially when they assume that they cannot communicate with their ELL students because they do not speak their students' first language. In actuality, the majority of the ELL students have developed a minimum repertoire of basic interpersonal communication skills that allow them to socialize and interact with their teachers, at least superficially (see Cummins, 2000).

Linguagrams are devices that allow educators to reason about their individual ELL students' proficiency in both English and their first language (Solano-Flores, 2012). They allow them to be mindful about the fact that ELL students' linguistic resources are not limited to English, to appreciate that a given ELL's language proficiency varies tremendously across language modes, and to see how each ELL student is unique as to their pattern of strengths and weaknesses in each language mode both in their first language and in English.

A *linguagram* is a symmetric bar graph that teachers construct by representing a subjective estimation of an ELL's proficiency in English and in their first language for each language mode—listening, reading, speaking, and writing (Figure 4.3). The lengths of the bars represent values of proficiency expressed in percentages,

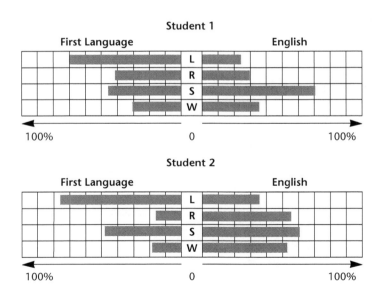

FIGURE 4.3 Linguagrams of two hypothetical ELL students. The bars show the estimated level of proficiency in both the first language (to the left) and English (to the right). Different patterns of proficiency across languages and across language modes can be appreciated. The patterns may differ across social contexts (e.g. at school, with friends).

ranging from 0 percent (total lack of proficiency) to 100 percent (full proficiency). Needless to say, the representation of 100 percent is conceptual since, as discussed above, strictly speaking, nobody is fully proficient in a language.

In order to serve its purpose as a conceptual tool for thinking about an ELL's language proficiency, a bar is to be filled out only when several sources of information or pieces of evidence exist on the student's proficiency in the corresponding language and language mode and the educator integrates that information. Among many others, potential sources include conversations with the student in English, information provided by parents, and information provided by other teachers.

Needless to say, none of these sources is perfect. For example, it is well known that self-reports may not reflect an ELL's actual proficiency in English. Due to the stigma associated with not being proficient in English and to the perceived low status of their native language in their schools (see Nieto & Bode, 2012), many ELLs may be hesitant to admit that they are proficient in their native language and may overstate their proficiency in English.

It is easy to realize, from attempting to fill out linguagrams, that rarely the judgments on someone's language proficiency consider different language modes in either English or the first language. Also, it is easy to realize that, when a judgment on language proficiency is made for a given student, rarely does the information that substantiates that judgment originate from direct social interaction with the student. Except for test scores, all the sources of information on language proficiency listed above are informal. Yet, used in combination, they can help educators develop a sense of each of their ELL students' skills in each language and the ways in which they can support these students.

Interpreting ELL Students' Writing

The use of students' responses in notebooks, assignments, or written classroom tests requires paying attention to writing language beyond superficial features. Based on superficial features of writing, educators may dismiss as incorrect the writing of their ELL students without attempting to make sense of them. In actuality, the chaotic appearance of many ELL students' writing is a natural indication of an ongoing process of second language spelling development. The fact that the spelling mistakes in English made by ELLs and native speakers of the same language follow a predictable pattern (see Fashola, Drum, Mayer, & Kang, 1996) is an indication that this language spelling development is taking place.

In the early stages of the process of second language spelling development, ELL students' spelling is heavily influenced by the phonology and the graphophonic rules of their first language (the set of conventions by which sounds are associated with certain letters), especially when the correspondence between letters and sounds is high in the first language (Genessee, Geva, Dressler, & Kamil, 2008). This process is natural; as their exposure to written English accumulates, ELL students develop strategies that allow them to rely more on the visual appearance of words than on the ways in which they appear to sound. Moreover, this process appears to be an indication of a process of organization of the experience with different systems of writing conventions. For example, there is evidence that children who are exposed to different writing systems (e.g. in English and Arabic or in English and Chinese) develop a wide repertoire of representational resources (Kenner & Kress, 2003).

Needless to say, due to the influences of the phonology and graphophonic rules of the first language, the patterns of spelling mistakes made by ELL students may be very different from the patterns of spelling mistakes made by native English users. Lack of familiarity with these patterns may lead some educators to interpret those mistakes as an indication of learning difficulties, such as dyslexia, and even to erroneously refer these students to special education programs.

Figure 4.4 shows the writing of a Grade 3 student from *Literacy Squared*, a project that investigates the development of reading and writing skills in students who receive instruction in both Spanish and English (Escamilla *et al.*, 2014). Clearly, the pattern of spelling mistakes is different from the pattern of spelling mistakes that would be observed in a monolingual, native English user. For example, the student writes *happen* instead of *happened*. For native users of some languages, phonetically, the *ed* is not clearly distinguishable at early stages of development of English as a second language. The word *guime* (in *my dad guime a pupy*) is more difficult to decode, but equally fascinating. First, not familiar with the fact that the verb, *give* is irregular, the student uses the regular past tense form (*gived*). Second, *gived* and *me* are written as a single word. Third, the *u* in *guived* follows a convention in written Spanish according to which the sound of the *g* in *gi* and *gui* is, respectively, as in *he* and *Gilmore*. All these mistakes are natural in the development of writing in English as a second language or in the development of biliteracy in two languages.

Aside from spelling and grammatical mistakes, the structure of the essay is coherent, and the ideas are well linked. Moreover, the story has a strong beginning, an interesting development, and an elegant ending. These important features cannot be appreciated if the assessment of the student's writing focuses only on superficial features. As proposed by Soltero-Gonzalez, Escamilla, and Hopewell (2012), a holistic lens of writing gives a more accurate view of the students' writing skills.

Write about the best thing that has ever happened to you. Why was it the best thing?

The best thing that happen to me is wen my dad guime a pupy. I laket sow much dad i bay him alot of clows, Toys and food. My pupy was brawn, big, nais and a lito fat. Do you luke how is my pupy? I forgot to say you dad his name was charo.

FIGURE 4.4 An essay from an emergent bilingual student. *The best thing that happened to me is when my dad gave me a puppy. I liked it so much that I bought him a lot of clothes, toys, and food. My puppy was brown, big, nice, and a little fat. Do you like how is my puppy? I forgot to say (to) you that his name was Charo.*

Closing Comments

English language arts, proficiency in English as a native language, English as a foreign language, and English as a second language are related but different domains. In selecting and using tests for assessing English proficiency among ELL students, it is important to make sure that these instruments are sensitive to the process of bilingual development and have been originally created for ELL populations.

As with any other test, English proficiency tests are not perfect instruments. Therefore, they can render erroneous classifications of students in different categories of English proficiency. To have an accurate idea of each of their ELL students' needs, educators should use different sources of information about their language proficiency in addition to the information provided by tests of English proficiency. No source of information is perfect; all possible sources should be used in combination. Direct social interaction with the students is essential for educators to have a good sense of their students' proficiency in English.

The patterns of spelling mistakes made by ELL students in their writing is different from the patterns of spelling mistakes observed among native English speakers. In ELL students, these patterns of spelling mistakes are heavily influenced by the phonology and graphophonic rules of their first languages. Educators should be aware of the reasons for these differences to avoid confusing limited proficiency in English with learning disabilities.

Exercises

Exercise 4.1: Language Proficiency as a Domain of Knowledge and Skills

1. Visit WIDA's English Language Development (ELD) Standards website (https://www.wida.us/standards/eld.aspx) and click on the links to the Performance Definitions for Listening and Reading, Grades K–12 and the Performance Definitions for Speaking and Writing, Grades K–12 (Note 4.1). Each document consists of a chart with the format shown in Figure 4.5, and which specifies:
    *   five levels of English proficiency: 1. Entering, 2. Emerging, 3. Developing, 4. Expanding, and 5. Bridging (a sixth level, Reaching, is used to represent the end of the development continuum); and
    *   three features of academic language: Discourse, Sentence, and Word/ Phrase (and their corresponding criteria, Linguistic Complexity, Language Forms, and Conventions).
2. Examine the performance descriptions provided in each cell for Listening and Reading and for Speaking and Writing. Then, based on your analysis and on the ideas discussed in the chapter, provide a definition of each of the

Level of English Proficiency	Features of Academic Language		
	Discourse Level	Sentence Level	Word/Phrase Level
	Linguistic Complexity	Language Forms and Conventions	Vocabulary Usage
	Level 6		
5			
4			
3			
2			
1			

FIGURE 4.5 Format for examining features of academic language by level of English proficiency according to the WIDA standards.

following terms, as they relate to listening and reading and as they relate to speaking and writing:

- Discourse
- Linguistic complexity
- Convention
- Academic language
- English proficiency

3. Based on your examination of the performance descriptions, is it possible for a given ELL student to have reached different levels of proficiency in English regarding linguistic complexity, language forms and conventions, and vocabulary usage across different social contexts? Discuss why and support your answer with examples from your experience with ELL students.

4. Reflect on your own teaching and assessment practices. Think how frequently you pay attention to the following aspects of language when you interact with your ELL students or when you examine their work.

- Vocabulary
- Spelling
- Pronunciation
- Grammatical structure
- Organization
- Discourse
- Complexity of ideas
- Strategic use of language (e.g. knowing how to use language to serve different communicative functions)

5. Do you think you pay equal attention to these different aspects of language? If not, why? What can you do to ensure you pay special attention to them? How can paying attention to multiple aspects of language contribute to improving the ways in which you support your ELL students?

Exercise 4.2: Comparing Language Tests

1. Visit Wikipedia and search for the following entry: "List of language proficiency tests." Click on the link, "English." A list of different tests of English proficiency will appear on your screen. Click on six to eight entries and browse through the descriptions.
2. Discuss your observations concerning the variety of English proficiency tests concerning:
    *   Target populations
    *   Contexts of usage of English
    *   Types of tasks used (e.g. types of items)
    *   Testing time
    *   Forms of grading or scoring
    *   Kinds of generalizations that are to be made about the test takers
    *   Purpose of the test (e.g. to hire employees)
    *   Importance given to each of the language modes—listening, reading, speaking, and writing
    *   Ways in which English proficiency is understood
    *   Process of test development
    *   Consistency across tests regarding the kind of information reported or made available to the public
3. Based on the comparison you made, which test strikes you as the one with the highest quality and which one strikes you as the one with the lowest quality? Justify your answers.

Exercise 4.3: Constructing Linguagrams

1. Select four ELL students randomly.
2. Using the format shown in Figure 4.6, fill out the linguagram for each of the four students. Draw a bar to indicate your overall judgment of the level of proficiency in each language mode in the first language and in English. Draw the bar only when you can make a judgment based on **at least three different** sources of information from the following list of sources:
    *   Test scores/test reports
    *   Information from the school district
    *   Conversations with the student in English

- Conversations with the students in their native language (only when the teacher speaks that language)
- Examining students' responses in notebooks or assignments
- Self-reports
- Observations of the student interacting with friends or peers
- Observations of the student interacting with parents
- Information provided by parents
- Information provided by other teachers

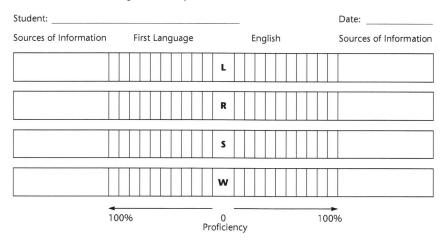

Student: _____   Date: _____

FIGURE 4.6   Format for composing linguagrams.

3. See the "Sources of Information" columns in the linguagram. For each language and language mode, in the appropriate cell, report the sources you used to make your judgments.

4. Based on comparing the four finished linguagrams, what commonalities and differences can you identify across the students' proficiency in their first language and in English? How is your view of the students' skills based on the linguagrams consistent with previous perceptions of the students' skills or from any information provided by tests? How consistent is the information you obtained from different sources? What are the limitations of each of the different sources of information you used?

Exercise 4.4: Decoding ELL Students' Written Responses

1. Read aloud the following essay by a Grade 3 student, and make an attempt to understand what is written. You may need to read the work several times; with a little perseverance, you should be able to make sense of the essay. The essay is from *Literacy Squared*, a research and intervention project that examines biliteracy development (Escamilla *et al.*, 2014).

Write about the best thing that has ever happened to you. Why was it the best thing?

The vest ting was tat in my hous ter was a big porti bicos my mom is guene hav ei bibe enets guene bi e boy en mien my famili or exairer cuas shi was habing a bebe pot they guift shus for the bebe en clous iben hats for the bebe tha en the mariachis queimen en they starer singuin for my mom en then we guif them ford end three pipo quimin in the hous en it hos my bes onclo my dad en my big frend end my dad en my onclo sed to look ausaid quos ther was a trampolin en ased tenquiu for the trampolin.

2. Write the "translation" of the essay. A translation of the essay is provided below, at the end of this exercise, for you to verify your work. However, do not use is it until you are you sure you have made your best to translate the essay.
3. Answer the following questions:
   - Can you identify any pattern or regularity in the spelling mistakes? Explain.
   - Putting aside the spelling and punctuation mistakes, what can you say about the quality of the essay, its structure, its development, its style, the sequence of ideas?
4. Provide a holistic evaluation of the essay.

Translation:
The best thing was that in my house there was a big party because my mom is going to have a baby and it's going to be a boy and me and my family are excited 'cause she was having a baby but they gived shoes for the baby and clothes, even hats for the baby. Then, and the mariachis came in and they started singing for my mom, and then we gived them food and three people came in the house and it was my best uncle, my dad and my big friend. And my dad and my uncle said to look outside 'cause there was a trampoline and I said thank you for the trampoline.

Note

Note 4.1. The charts can also be found in WIDA (2012).

References

Abedi, J. (2007). English language learners with disabilities. In C. C. Laitusis & L. L. Cook (Eds.), *Large-scale assessment and accommodation: What works* (pp. 23–35). Arlington, VA: Council for Exceptional Children.

Artiles, A. J., Trent, S. C., & Palmer, J. (2004). Culturally diverse students in special education: Legacies and prospects. In J. A. Banks & C. M. Banks (Eds.), *Handbook of research on multicultural education, second edition* (pp. 716–735). San Francisco: Jossey-Bass.

August, D. & Hakuta, K. (Eds.) (1997). *Improving schooling for language minority students: A research agenda.* Committee on Developing a Research Agenda on the Education of Limited-English-Proficient and Bilingual Students, Board on Children, Youth, and Families, Commission on Behavioral and Social Sciences and Education, National Research Council, Institute of Medicine. Washington, DC: National Academy Press.

August, D. & Shanahan, T. (Eds.) (2006). *Developing literacy in second-language learners: Report of the National Literacy Panel on Language-Minority Children and Youth.* Mahwah, NJ: Lawrence Erlbaum Associates, Inc., Publishers.

Bialystok, E. (2001). *Bilingualism in development: Language, literacy, and cognition.* Cambridge, UK: Cambridge University Press.

Cheatham, G. A., Jimenez-Silva, M. Wodrich, D. L., & Kasai, M. (2014). Disclosure of information about English proficiency: Preservice teachers' presumptions about English language learners. *Journal of Teacher Education, 65*(1), 53–62.

Council of Chief State School Officers (2012). *Framework for English language proficiency development standards corresponding to the Common Core State Standards and the Next Generation Science Standards.* Washington, DC: CCSSO.

Cummins, J. (2000). *Language, power, and pedagogy: Bilingual children in the crossfire.* Clevedon, England: Multilingual Matters Ltd.

Escamilla, K. (2000). Bilingual means two: Assessment issues, early literacy and Spanish speaking children. *Reading Research Symposium for Second Language Learners.* Washington, DC: National Clearinghouse for Bilingual Education.

Escamilla, K., Hopewell, S., Butvilofsky, S., Sparrow, W., Soltero-Gonzalez, L. Ruiz Figueroa, O., & Escamilla, M. (2014) *Biliteracy from the start: Literacy Squared in action.* Philadelphia, PA: Caslon Publishing.

Fashola, O., Drum, P., Mayer, R., & Kang, S. (1996). A cognitive theory of orthographic transitioning: Predictable errors in how Spanish-speaking children spell English words. *American Educational Research Journal, 33*(4), 825–843.

García, G. E., McKoon, G., & August, D. (2006). Language and literacy assessment of language-minority students. In D. August & T. Shanahan (Eds.), *Developing literacy in second-language learners: report of the National Literacy Panel on Language-Minority Children and Youth* (pp. 597–626). Mahwah, NJ: Lawrence Erlbaum Associates, Inc., Publishers.

Gass, S. & Selinker, L. (2001). *Second language acquisition: An introduction, second edition*. Mahwah, NJ: Lawrence Erlbaum Associates, Publishers.

Genesee, F., Geva, E., Dressler, C., & Kamil, M. L. (2008). Cross-linguistic relationships in second-language learners. In D. August & T. Shanahan (Eds.), *Developing reading and writing in second-language learners* (pp. 61–93). New York: Routledge.

Grosjean, F. (1989). Neurolinguists, beware! The bilingual is not two monolinguals in one person. *Brain and Language, 36*, 3–15.

Hakuta, K. (2000). *How long does it take English learners to attain proficiency?* University of California Linguistic Minority Research Institute. Policy Reports. Santa Barbara: Linguistic Minority Research Institute. Retrieved July 28, 2009 from http://repositories.cdlib.org/lmri/pr/hakuta.

Hakuta, K. (2015). How is English language proficiency assessed under the Common Core State Standards, and how can we use these data to inform and improve instruction? In G. Valdés, K. Menken, & M. Castro (Eds.), *Common Core, bilingual and English language learners: A resource for educators* (p. 252). Philadelphia, PA: Caslon, Inc.

Hopewell, S. & Escamilla, K. (2013). Struggling reader or emerging biliterate student? Reevaluating the criteria for labeling emerging bilingual students as low achieving. *Journal of Literacy Research, 46*(1), 68–89.

Kenner, C. & Kress, G. (2003). The multisemiotic resources of biliterate children. *Journal of Early Childhood Literacy, 3*(2), 179–202.

Klingner J. & Harry, B. (2006). The special education referral and decision-making process for English language learners: Child study team meetings and placement conferences. *Teachers College Record, 108*(11), 2247–2281.

MacSwan, J. (2000). The threshold hypothesis, semilingualism, and other contributions to a deficit view of linguistic minorities. *Hispanic Journal of Behavioral Sciences, 22*(1), 3–45.

MacSwan, J. & Rolstad, K. (2006). How language proficiency tests mislead us about ability: Implications for English language learner placement in special education. *Teachers College Record, 108*(11), 2304–2328.

Nieto, S. & Bode, P. (2012). *Affirming diversity: The sociocultural context of multicultural education, 6th edition*. Boston: Pearson.

Oller, D. K., Pearson, B. Z., & Cobo-Lewis, A. B. (2007). Profile effects in early bilingual language and literacy. *Applied Psycholinguistics, 28*, 191–230.

Raizen, S. A. (1997). *Standards for science education*. Occasional Paper No. 1. Madison, WI: National Institute for Science Education, University of Wisconsin–Madison and National Center for Improving Science Education.

Solano-Flores, G. (2011). *Assessing the cultural validity of assessment practices: An introduction*. In M. R. Basterra, E. Trumbull, & G. Solano-Flores (Eds.), *Cultural validity in assessment: Addressing linguistic and cultural diversity* (pp. 3–21). New York: Routledge.

Solano-Flores, G. (2012). *Translation accommodations framework for testing English language learners in mathematics*. Developed for the Smarter Balanced Assessment Consortium (SBAC). September 18, 2012.

Soltero-González, L., Escamilla, K., & Hopewell, S. (2012). Changing teachers' perceptions about the writing abilities of emerging bilingual students: Toward a holistic bilingual perspective on writing assessment. *International Journal of Bilingual Education and Bilingualism, 15*(1), 71–94.

Valdés, G. & Figueroa, R. A. (1994). *Bilingualism and testing: A special case of bias*. Norwood, NJ: Ablex.

Walqui, A. (2015). What to educators need to know about language as they make decisions about Common Core State Standards implementation? In G. Valdés, K. Menken, & M. Castro (Eds.), *Common Core, bilingual and English language learners: A resource for educators* (p. 49–50). Philadelphia, PA: Caslon, Inc.

WIDA (World-Class Instructional Design and Assessment) (2012). Amplification of the English Language Development Standards: Kindergarten–Grade 12. Wisconsin: Board of Regents of the University of Wisconsin System.

5

ASSESSING CONTENT KNOWLEDGE

Overview

This chapter discusses the process of development of instruments intended to assess content knowledge in both the context of large-scale assessment and the classroom context. Also, it offers ideas for teachers to make assessment work in the benefit of their instruction.

The section "How Large-Scale Tests Are Made" discusses the process of test development in large-scale assessment programs. Critical to this process is the view of assessment as a sample of tasks.

The section "Using Assessment Beyond Grading" discusses how, in order to benefit from assessment, educators need to be able to establish meaningful relationships between the content of tests and the content of their teaching. Teaching practices should not be influenced solely by the content of the items of standardized tests, which are limited in their sensitivity to instruction and the experiences that take place in the classroom.

The section "Developing Classroom Performance Assessments" discusses why it is important for educators to be able to create their own assessments. Performance assessments are discussed as resources of great instructional value. The section also discusses the value of developing assessments as a professional development experience that opens doors for opportunities for collaboration with colleagues.

How Large-Scale Tests Are Made

Tests as Samples of Observations

As discussed in Chapter 1, sampling is the process throughout which a portion of a whole is examined with the intent to make generalizations about the characteristics of a population or universe (the whole) based on the characteristics of the sample. Also as mentioned in Chapter 1, *sample*, *population*, and *universe* are not terms that refer exclusively to persons.

In the context of large-scale assessment, a test can be viewed as a sample of tasks that are intended to represent the universe of concepts, problems, and situations that compose a domain of knowledge and skills. More specifically, a test can be viewed as a sample of observations (Cronbach, Gleser, Nanda, & Rajaratnam, 1972; Kane, 1982, 2006). Based on the performance of students on different tasks, generalizations are made about their knowledge and skills in a given content area.

Knowledge Domain Specification

The view of tests as samples helps to understand the importance of properly specifying the domain of knowledge and skills to be assessed. Properly specifying that domain allows identification of the content of interest (e.g. different topics) and the different types of knowledge (e.g. declarative, procedural, schematic, and strategic) to be assessed with the items of a test.

Knowledge domain specification is the description of a domain of knowledge or skills in a way that enables test developers to systematically draw (generate) tasks from it. Knowledge domains are typically infinite. Think, for example, of all the possible problems, situations and contexts that constitute a domain such as *oral communication* or *mathematical reasoning*. Because of this vastness, enumerating all possible problems, situations, and contexts that compose a domain of knowledge and skills would not be a practical approach to draw items from it. A more effective strategy consists of specifying the domain according to a reduced number of categories of tasks to which all the possible tasks may belong. This is done based on knowledge on the content to be assessed and, in the case of large-scale assessment, based on normative documents, such as standards documents.

Figure 5.1 illustrates how a domain is specified. The example is taken from a document commissioned by the National Assessment Governing Board (2008) developed to support test developers to generate items for the National Assessment of Educational Progress 2009 science assessment. This document was, in turn, aligned with the national science education standards (National Research Council, 1996).

The design of the assessment was guided based on the intersection of science content and science practices. A science content statement was written as a performance expectation in the cell resulting from the intersection of a content area

			Content Area		
			Physical science content statements	Life science content statements	Earth and space science content statements
Science practices	Knowing science	Identifying science principles			
		Using science principles			
	Doing science	Using scientific inquiry			
		Using technological design			

FIGURE 5.1 A content matrix for a science test. Adapted from National Assessment Governing Board (2008).

(physical science, life science, or earth and space science) and a science practice (identifying science principles, using science principles, using scientific inquiry, or using technological design). For example, the performance expectation for Grade 8, Physical Science, Identifying Science Principles was:

> Identify the units that might be used to measure the speed of an ant and the speed of an airplane. (p. 139)

Likewise, the performance expectation for Grade 8, Earth and Space Science, Using Scientific Inquiry was:

> Given data (indexed by month) on annual trends of incoming solar radiation for five cities, determine whether the location is in the Northern or Southern Hemisphere. (p. 139)

The test developers' job was to create items for each performance expectation. It should be obvious that multiple-choice and short-answer items tend to be appropriate for assessing "knowing science" whereas constructed-response tasks (e.g. essays, experiments) tend to be appropriate for assessing "doing science."

Given their influential role in the process of assessment, ideally, standards documents should provide a comprehensive view of language and its relationship with disciplinary knowledge. This characteristic would guide test developers in their efforts to address language issues since the inception of any assessment. This ideal is consistent with the notion that genuine inclusion of ELLs in the process of assessment cannot take place if these students are not taken into consideration throughout the entire process of assessment development (see Kopriva, 2008; Trumbull & Solano-Flores, 2011).

Unfortunately, standards documents tend to address language and linguistic groups as a topic in a special section rather than an issue that cuts across all topics. Criticisms to some standards documents point at limitations in addressing the relationship of everyday language and academic language as critical to the construction of knowledge (Barwell, 2005) and at the use of an assimilationist perspective regarding linguistic and cultural minorities (Lee, 1999).

Types and Numbers of Items

Theory, logical reasoning, and practical constraints shape the content and number of tasks included in large-scale tests. While a matrix like that shown in Figure 5.1 allows systematic identification of the items that need to be developed, other factors influence the final configuration of an assessment. For instance, content standards and other normative documents may emphasize certain content areas or types of knowledge over others. Also, the development, administration, and scoring may be more costly for some tasks than others. This poses a limit to the number of constructed-response tasks that can be included in a test.

In large-scale tests, the number of items needed to properly sample a large knowledge domain is much greater than the number of items that is reasonable to give students in a test booklet. It is not uncommon that over 100 items have to be created for a single test for a given grade and content area (e.g. Grade 4 mathematics) in a given year (e.g. NAEP, 2010), whereas the test booklets given to students cannot have more than about 40 items. Since it is not possible or recommendable to give many items to students, the assessment has to be administered to students in different *blocks* of items. In this arrangement, there may be several blocks with different combinations of items, although some items are common across blocks. This kind of test allows making generalizations about a population's (not individual students') knowledge and skills (see Mazzeo, Lazer, & Zieky, 2006).

Item specifications are documents used by large-scale assessment programs intended to guide the development of test items. These documents support test developers in creating all the items needed according to a predetermined set of characteristics such as format, problem structure, problem complexity, type of contextual information, and the characteristics of illustrations (see Downing, 2006).

The importance of item specifications documents cannot be understated. They ensure standardization in the process of test development beyond the idiosyncratic preferences and styles of item writers, and ensure that the items generated assess the target knowledge and skills (Baker, 2007). Detailed and clear item specifications contribute to ensuring that any student performance differences across items that assess the same content are due to differences in the knowledge of that content, rather than differences in items' characteristics that are not related to that content.

Ideally, as part of their process of development, test items are tried out several times with samples of pilot students to determine if students interpret the items as the developers intend and to refine the items' wording when needed (Solano-Flores & Shavelson, 1977). This information is collected through examination of the students' responses and from interviews, verbal protocols, and other procedures intended to probe understanding.

Appropriate representation of ELLs in the samples of students who participate in this stage of the process should ensure that these modifications in the wording of items are sensitive to the characteristics of ELL students. There is evidence that substantial proportions of ELL students have the minimum proficiency in English needed for them to participate in interviews conducted in English and to provide valuable information about the ways in which they interpret test items administered in English (Prosser & Solano-Flores, 2010). Yet, unfortunately, including ELL students in the entire process of development of large-scale tests is yet to become standard practice.

Using Assessment Beyond Grading

Educators need to use information from standardized tests judiciously, in ways that inform—rather than dictate—their instruction. Three conditions are important for educators to accomplish such a goal: knowing how different types of tasks are sensitive to different types of knowledge, understanding the limitations of teaching to the test, and being mindful of the instructional sensitivity of large-scale tests as key to properly interpreting the information produced by these instruments.

Types of Tasks and Types of Knowledge

As discussed in detail in Chapter 1, assessment can be viewed as a process of reasoning from evidence collected with the purpose of drawing inferences about the students' knowledge or skills (Pellegrino, Chudowsky, & Glaser, 2001). According to this view, an assessment instrument is "a tool designed to observe students' behavior and produce data that can be used to draw reasonable inferences about what students know" (p. 42). Also according to that view, any assessment is based on three elements:

> *Cognition*—a conception of the cognitive processes underlying student performance (e.g. ways in which students represent knowledge and develop competencies in a given knowledge domain).

Observation—a conception of the tasks that will elicit the behavior that demonstrates if the student has the knowledge or skills being assessed.

Interpretation—an approach for interpreting information obtained from the tasks as evidence of the knowledge or skills being assessed.

Cognition, observation, and interpretation are reflected, respectively in the types of knowledge the tasks included in a test are intended to assess (e.g. declarative, procedural, schematic, strategic knowledge), the characteristics of the tasks and response formats included in a test (e.g. restricted- and constructed-response), and the set of rules for scoring performance based on the quality or correctness of the students' responses (e.g. correct–incorrect, partial credit).

Figure 5.2 shows the relationship between the level of openness of different types of tasks and the types of knowledge to which they tend to be sensitive. *Openness* refers to the extent to which a task allows students to construct and provide their responses in multiple ways. It has to be said that the figure is not intended to represent clear-cut differences between the sensitivity of different types of tasks. The relationships represented may vary depending on how these

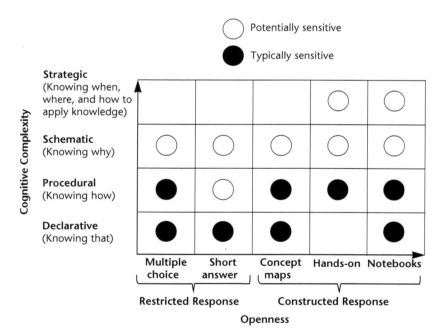

FIGURE 5.2 Different types of assessment tasks (arranged by level of openness) and their range of sensitivity to different types of knowledge (arranged by level of cognitive complexity). Black and white circles represent, respectively, the types of knowledge to which each type of task is typically and potentially (or less frequently) sensitive.

different broad task categories are defined and understood. For example, what counts as a "concept map" or "hands-on task" or "portfolio" may vary tremendously across teachers or test developers and so may their common or potential sensitivity to different types of knowledge.

Restricted-response tasks such as multiple-choice and short-answer items are predominantly sensitive to declarative and procedural knowledge. They involve skills such as information recognition, fact recall, and the application of existing procedures or sequence of steps. The variety of ways in which students can provide their responses is limited. These responses consist, for example, of selecting one option among three or four options, or completing a sentence with a word or a few words. Typically, students' responses are scored dichotomously (correct–incorrect).

Constructed-response tasks such as concept maps, hands-on tasks, and notebooks tend to be sensitive to procedural knowledge and, potentially, schematic and strategic knowledge. They involve skills such as integration of information, problem solving, and critical thinking, and are amenable to a wide variety of approaches and solutions. The response formats allow students to provide their responses in multiple ways, for example by reporting results with drawings and using their own words. Students' responses can be scored using partial-credit models. These scoring models take into consideration the level of quality of both the product (outcome) of the students' actions and the processes by which students arrive at their solutions. Constructed-response assessments are sometimes referred to as "authentic assessments" because they tend to pose problems that are representative of real-life problems and situations.

The distinction between types of knowledge to which tasks are typically sensitive and types of knowledge to which tasks are potentially (or less frequently) sensitive recognizes the fact that, if properly developed, tasks with low levels of openness can be rich and cognitive demanding. Indeed, multiple-choice items can be crafted that elicit complex thinking (Martinez, 1999; Thissen-Roe, Hunt, & Minstrell, 2004). To illustrate this, compare the following items:

1. Which number is the product of 414/23?
   A. 14
   B. 16
   C. 18
2. In the division $W = X / Y$, W will be >1 if
   A. $Y < X, Y \neq 0$, and $X \neq 0$
   B. $Y > X, Y \neq 0$, and $X \neq 0$
   C. $Y = X, Y \neq 0$, and $X \neq 0$

To respond correctly to Item 1, students need to perform an operation according to an algorithm and then compare the result to the values shown by the options. In contrast, to respond correctly to Item 2, students need to make an abstraction of the operation—what a division is—based on their experience performing divisions. While Item 1 can be thought of as being mainly sensitive to procedural knowledge (knowing how), Item 2 can be thought of as being mainly sensitive to schematic knowledge (knowing why) and, therefore, as being also more cognitively demanding.

Limitations of Teaching to the Test

Large-scale tests are intended to provide information on the extent to which learning goals are met. Yet, due to the serious consequences attached to them, they end up driving the content taught in class (see Shepard, 2010). While teaching to the test is common, the practice may not be entirely effective or adaptive (Popham, 2001). As discussed above, tests are samples of a domain of knowledge and skills. As Figure 5.3 shows, by teaching to the test, teachers focus on a sample of domain of knowledge and skills rather than on the entire domain. In addition, because tests tend to contain considerably more tasks of low openness than tasks of high openness, test-driven teaching may overemphasize declarative and procedural knowledge over schematic and strategic knowledge. Moreover, when teachers teach to the test, they may develop inaccurate perceptions of the extent to which their students meet the learning goals (see Sloane & Kelly, 2003).

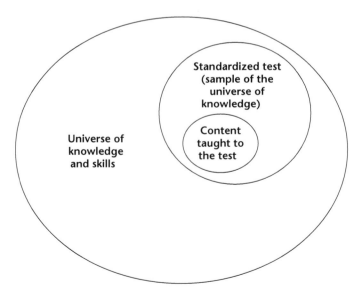

FIGURE 5.3 Teaching to the test from a sampling perspective. The content taught when teachers teach to the test is a sample of the possible content assessed by a large-scale test—which in turn is a sample of the target universe of knowledge and skills.

Instructional Sensitivity

Large-scale tests provide information meaningful to instruction to the extent that they are sensitive to the enacted curriculum—the ways in which teachers implement the planned ("official, written") curriculum through their instruction (Ruiz-Primo, Shavelson, Hamilton, & Klein, 2002). Because school district, state, and national tests are developed in alignment with standards documents, the goals they address (what knowledge or skills students should be able to demonstrate), their content (e.g. topics, procedures), and the nature of their tasks and items are unlikely to reflect entirely the specific lessons and topics taught and the specific tasks, activities, and materials used in a specific classroom. Compared to classroom assessment activities, the instructional sensitivity of state and national large-scale tests is limited because those instruments are distant from the specific experiences that take place in the classroom. While large-scale tests produce valuable information about academic achievement, they cannot be expected to produce all the information teachers need to properly support their students.

Research on instructional sensitivity and the distance of assessments to the enacted curriculum has not addressed language sufficiently. Yet it is not difficult to view language as an important part of the sets of experiences that take place in the classroom. Also, it is not difficult to understand the limited sensitivity of large-scale tests to the ways in which language is used to implement curriculum in the classrooms. Only classroom-based assessments are sensitive to the sets of experiences, topics, activities, materials and forms of language usage that are specific to the curriculum enacted in the classroom.

Developing Classroom Performance Assessments

Due to the increasing impact of large-scale testing and accountability on the lives of teachers, their students, and their schools, current expectations for teachers to develop their own assessment instruments and activities may be lower than any other time in history. Educators may pay attention to assessments only when they are required to test their students and grading may be the main function served by tests. In addition, educators may not find reasons why they should spend time developing assessments for their students when there are many assessments commercially available or available online. Also, engaging in assessment development activities may not be appealing to many educators in times in which large-scale testing and test-preparation activities consume already a sizeable amount of their time.

The reasons in support of teachers developing their own assessments become obvious when assessments are thought of as instructional tools. The attention paid by this section to performance assessments is based on the premise that using these assessments as instructional tools expands the range of resources educators can use to effectively support their students' learning. As Table 5.1 shows, constructed-response assessment is consistent with a constructivist perspective of teaching.

TABLE 5.1 Correspondence of Constructivist Views of Teaching and the Intended Characteristics of Performance Assessments.

Dimension	Teaching	Assessment
Student's Role	Students are regarded as active (not passive) learners.	Students develop their own problem-solving strategies and provide responses in their own words.
Activities	Activities are intended to promote meaning-making and the construction of knowledge.	Tasks are intended to reflect real-life situations and meaningful contexts.
Knowledge	Knowledge is viewed as imprecise but perfectible.	Tasks admit to a wide range of solutions with varying levels of correctness.
Process of Learning	Making mistakes is part of the process of learning.	Scoring considers both the quality of the response and the quality of the problem-solving approach used.

Instructional Value

High-quality constructed-response assessments have an intrinsic pedagogical value (Shavelson, 1995) and elicit higher-order thinking skills (e.g. problem solving, evaluation, critical thinking) (Darling-Hammond & Adamson, 2010). To a large extent, their instructional value stems from the fact that they elicit the cognitive integration of different pieces of information in meaningful contexts.

Take as an example *Daytime Astronomy Shadows*, a fifth-grade hands-on assessment (Figure 5.4) created to assess knowledge on the movement of the earth and the sun (Solano-Flores & Shavelson, 1997).

Two pieces of declarative knowledge are needed to respond correctly to answer correctly to Questions 2 (*How do the shadows of Tower A look at 10 a.m. and at 3 p.m.?*) and 3 (*Do sun shadows move and change the same way in the northern and southern hemispheres?*). One is that the earth spins from west to east; the other is that, roughly, the sun's light is perpendicular to the earth's surface at the equator. Practically every student knows these two facts. Yet students need to think carefully about them before they can provide their answers. Modeling the rotation of the earth and the sun's light on the equator allows students to use and relate the two pieces of declarative knowledge and see how they work in combination to explain a process.

Day Time Astronomy (Shadows)

Equipment:
- **Spinning** Earth globe in a box
- Flashlight
- Sticky towers A, B, and C

There are three towers of the same height in the **United States: A, B, and C.**
Put Towers **A** and **B** on the globe, where indicated (they will stick). Use the flashlight as
if it is the sun. At noon, the shadows of Towers **A** and **B** should look like this:

We don't know where in the United States Tower **C** is. We only know that when it's noon for
Towers **A** and **B**, the shadow of Tower **C** looks like this:

Use the flashlight as if it is the sun. You may try as many places as you need.

Questions:
1. Where in the United States is Tower **C**? How did you find out?
2. How do the shadows of **Tower A** look at 10 a.m. and at 3 p.m.?
3. Do sun shadows move and change the same way in the northern and southern hemispheres?

FIGURE 5.4 In the Daytime Astronomy (Shadows) assessment, students are given an earth globe encased in a box, sticky towers that they can position and reposition on the globe, and a flashlight. Students model the movement of the earth by spinning the globe and use the flashlight to model the sun's light. The figure shows excerpts from the assessment booklet. The text and the format have been edited to fit the size of the figure.

From the actions students take to complete this task, teachers can determine if the modeling reflects the use of the two pieces of declarative knowledge. For example: Do the students make their observations spinning the earth globe from west to east? Do they orient the flashlight to the equator or somewhere else (e.g. right above the tower)? The activity is engaging and promotes discussion among students when they work in pairs. Based on the conversations students have while they are engaged in solving the problems, teachers develop a sense of the ideas and concepts that need to be discussed in detail.

Devising a Performance Assessment

As a starting point in the process of developing their own assessments, educators can ask questions like the following with regard to a unit or lesson:

- What would I like my students to be able to do to demonstrate that they have learned key knowledge and skills form the unit or lesson?

- What is a problem not seen in class whose solution requires applying the knowledge and skills learned in that unit or lesson?
- What ideas, concepts, and skills should my students be able to use in combination in order to solve that problem correctly?

The assessment needs to have three components (Ruiz-Primo & Shavelson, 1996):

- a problem which can be solved using in different ways;
- a response format—a medium for capturing information on both the students' problem solving activities and the outcomes of those actions (e.g. a booklet with questions and space for students to report their actions, the rationale for those actions, and the results obtained); and
- a scoring rubric—a system that identifies different sets of possible actions students may take to solve the problem and which assigns scores to those actions and their outcomes according to their correctness and soundness.

Of the three components, the response format is of particular interest in the assessment of ELL students because a great deal of the process of developing an assessment concerns refining its wording to ensure that students understand what they need to do and the kind of information they are required to report.

Iterative Development Process

Developing a constructed-response assessment is an iterative (cyclical) process, as shown in Figure 5.5. In a first iteration, an initial version of the task and the response format is tried out with a sample of students to determine if the level of difficulty and the wording are grade- and age-appropriate and to investigate the kind of knowledge and reasoning students use when they complete the task. For example, educators can listen to the conversations of students working in pairs. Also, teachers can have some students read aloud the directions of the task and think aloud while they complete the task individually. Also, teachers can perform short individual interviews with some students and ask them to describe what they think and do to figure out their responses.

These observations allow identification of aspects in which the assessment needs to be improved. For example, these observations may reveal that some students are able to solve the problem without using the knowledge and reasoning that the assessment is supposed to assess (Baxter & Glaser, 1998). Or, these observations may allow identification of words that are difficult to understand or phrases that are frequently misunderstood and mislead the students' actions. Or, students may come up with solution strategies that were not anticipated and need to be incorporated in the scoring system.

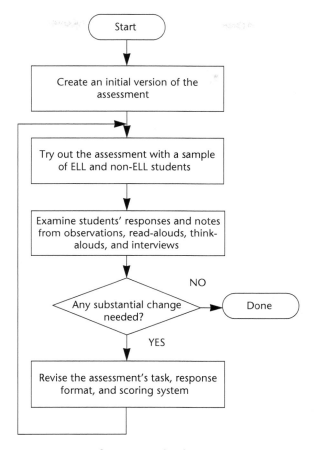

FIGURE 5.5 Iterative process of assessment development.

Based on these observations, the task, the response format, and the scoring system of the assessment are revised dynamically. Any modification on any of the three assessment components (task, response format, and scoring system) has implications on the characteristics of the other two components, which need to be revised accordingly. For example, modifying the wording of a question in the response format may need to be followed by modifications in the scoring system, as the change may affect the range of possible responses to that question. Or, in improving the scoring rubric based on examining the students' responses, the teacher may realize that the task can be improved by adding, eliminating, or modifying certain pieces of equipment or by making changes in the ways in which information is provided.

In further iterations, revised versions of the assessment are tried out with new samples of students and further improvements are made. It is important to ensure that ELL students participate in all the iterations of the process of assessment development.

The iterative process continues until no substantial changes on the task, the response format, or the scoring system are needed. A reasonable quality has been reached when the assessment:

- presents a context that is meaningful to the students;
- is challenging, engaging, and has an intrinsic instructional value;
- is amenable to multiple solutions and problem solving strategies varying in quality; and
- the scoring rubric captures a good variety of student types of responses.

Assessment Development as Professional Development

While some performance assessments are relatively easy to develop, others are more complex and may take much more time and several development iterations before a final version is reached. This should not discourage teachers from creating their own assessments, as the sole process of assessment development has an intrinsic great value as professional development activity (Arter, 1999; Darling-Hammond & Adamson, 2010).

As with lesson plans, teachers can refine their assessments over time, based on the experience they gain each time they use them. Teachers who teach several groups of students have the opportunity to try out and revise an assessment several times during the same school year. In contrast, teachers who teach one group of students during the school year may have the opportunity to try out and revise a given assessment only once a year. In both cases, teachers benefit from the iterative process of assessment development in various ways. First, they gain knowledge on the students thinking and reasoning that informs their teaching. Second, they develop a deeper understanding of the topic as they take actions to refine their assessments. Third, they develop more accurate and sophisticated views of language and culture as their refine the wording of their assessments (Solano-Flores, Trumbull, & Nelson-Barber, 2001).

An important way in which teachers benefit from developing their own assessments is that, as they make efforts to come up with ideas for tasks, they also develop a critical view of the curriculum they teach. For instance, to answer the questions listed in the subsection "Devising a Performance Assessment" above, teachers may need to examine a lesson from the perspective of assessment—rather than the perspective of instruction. It is not uncommon for teachers engaged in this endeavor to find ways in which a unit or lesson can be improved, for example by revising the sequence in which certain concepts are taught (Shavelson, 1995).

Appreciating the value of assessment development as an activity that promotes professional development opens the opportunity for collaboration among colleagues. In an ideal situation, teachers exchange ideas for classroom-based assessment and review and critique each other's assessments. As a group, teachers develop a bank of assessments that meet their instructional needs and are created to serve the population of students they teach. This form of collaboration helps teachers to appropriate assessment as a key activity in their profession.

Closing Comments

In both large-scale assessment and classroom contexts, the views of assessment as a process of reasoning from evidence and the view of assessment as a sample of observations, are critical to drawing accurate conclusions about the students' skills and knowledge. In large-scale assessment, properly specifying the domain of knowledge and skills is key to creating tasks that are representative of that domain. Ultimately, proper knowledge domain specification is central to the validity of a test.

In order to use information on student academic achievement provided by large-scale tests properly in ways that benefit their instruction, teachers need to be knowledgeable of the fact that different types of tasks tend to be sensitive to different types of knowledge. Also, they need to be aware of the fact that teaching to the test limits the quality of instruction. In order to properly interpret scores and information from large-scale tests, educators need to be aware of the fact that these instruments are limited in their sensitivity to the characteristics of the enacted curriculum (the kinds of activities, materials that take place in a specific classroom, and the ways in which language is used).

Developing their own assessments helps the teacher to refine their teaching skills. Performance assessments are particularly important because they are potentially effective teaching resources. Assessment development activities have a great value as professional development activities. While developing performance assessments is time consuming, this process of development can be viewed as a long-term project. Through the iterations in which draft versions of the assessments are tried out and revised, teachers can learn a great deal about their students and about the topics they teach. The importance of including ELL students in all stages of this iterative process of assessment development cannot be understated. The participation of these students contributes to ensuring that the assessments are properly worded, minimizing unnecessary linguistic demands beyond the linguistic demands that are intrinsic to the constructs assessed.

Exercises

Exercise 5.1: Using Students' Responses to Develop Multiple-Choice Items

1. Create an open-ended item on the topic of your choice. The topic should be a topic you know well and like to teach. It should target schematic knowledge (knowing why). It should involve bodies of knowledge (e.g. schemas,

mental models, or implicit or explicit "theories" for organizing information in ways that allows application of principles or models to provide explanations and make predictions).

2. Give the item to half of your students or, if possible, to students from another class but in the same grade. As with any teaching or assessment activity, be sure to include ELL students in your sample.

3. Examine the students' responses carefully. Regardless of whether the responses are correct or incorrect, try to identify the kinds of reasoning, knowledge, beliefs, conceptions, or mental models that the responses appear to reflect. If necessary, ask the students to verbally clarify or elaborate on their responses, so that you can obtain more information on their thinking. Based on this judgment, classify the responses into three or four groups, according to their similarities and differences.

4. Create the multiple-choice version of the open-ended item. Create the options of this multiple-choice item based on the three or four groups of responses you made before. For each group, create an option intended to capture the kinds of reasoning, knowledge, beliefs, conceptions, or mental models reflected by the responses.

5. Try the multiple-choice item several times with your students to make sure all of them understand the item.

6. How does creating options based on actual students' responses contribute to developing high-quality multiple-choice items that provide valuable information about the students' thinking? How is including ELL students in the process beneficial to them and to the process of development of test items?

Exercise 5.2: Representing a Knowledge Domain

1. Make a chart, diagram, or any other representational devise that shows the structure of the universe of multiplication operation problems.

2. Using your chart or diagram, identify the different types or classes of items that you could write for a test on multiplication operations.

3. Discuss how you can test whether the chart or diagram represents all the types or classes of multiplication problems.

Exercise 5.3: Scoring and Students' Reasoning

1. "Bubbles" is a Grade 4 assessment intended to assess science process skills in relation to the concepts of force and motion (Solano-Flores, 2000). See the prompt and the picture in Figure 5.6. Students conduct an experiment to determine which of three soapy solutions makes the most and the least durable bubbles. Equipment for making bubbles includes straws, syringes, and basters—all in sets of three pieces. These pieces of equipment vary in their

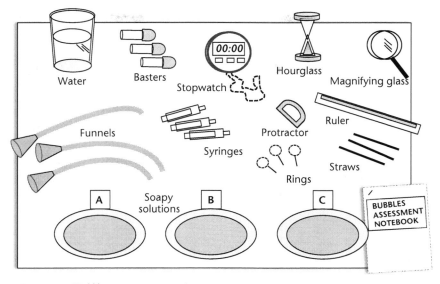

FIGURE 5.6 *Bubbles* assessment equipment.

effectiveness to make bubbles of the same size. Equipment for measuring time includes a stopwatch and an hourglass. The equipment also includes a protractor and a ruler—which are irrelevant to the solution of the problem and are intended to act as distractors. Making bubbles of the same size, measuring time with precision, and not mixing solutions are critical to conducting a successful experiment.

2. What kinds of reasoning do students need to use to conduct a sound experiment?
3. What rules would you use to score the students' responses?

Exercise 5.4: Cognitive and Linguistic Demands of Items

1. Observe the item below. The item is related to the concepts of force and motion.

Which of the following is the most important factor involved in the formation of a bubble?

A. gravity
B. viscosity
C. surface tension
D. density

---

2. What type of knowledge does the item assess? What kinds of reasoning do students need to use to respond to it correctly?
3. What rules are needed to score the students' responses?
4. Discuss any differences and commonalities between the prompt of the "Bubbles" assessment (see Exercise 5.3) and this item regarding cognitive demands.
5. Discuss any differences and commonalities between the prompt of the "Bubbles" assessment (see Exercise 5.3) and this item regarding linguistic demands.
6. Discuss how any differences and commonalities in the cognitive and linguistic demands between the two types of tasks are relevant to properly assessing ELL students.

References

Arter, J. (1999). Teaching about performance assessment. *Educational Measurement: Issues and Practice, 18*(2), 30–44.

Baker, E. L. (2007). Model-based assessments to support learning and accountability: The evolution of CRESST's research on multiple-purpose measures. *Educational Assessment, 12*(3 & 4), 179–194.

Barwell, R. (2005). Ambiguity in the mathematics classroom. *Language and Education, 19*(2), 118–126.

Baxter, G. P. & Glaser, R. (1998). Investigating the cognitive complexity of science assessments. *Educational Measurement: Issues and Practice, 17*(3), 37–45.

Cronbach, L. J., Gleser, G. C., Nanda, H., & Rajaratnam, N. (1972). *The dependability of behavioral measurements.* New York: Wiley.

Darling-Hammond, L. & Adamson, F. (2010). *Beyond basic skills: The role of performance assessment in achieving 21st century standards of learning.* Stanford, CA: Stanford University, Stanford Center for Opportunity Policy in Education.

Downing, S. M. (2006). Twelve steps for effective test development. In S. M. Downing & T. M. Haladyna (Eds.), *Handbook of test development* (pp. 3–25). Mahwah, NJ: Lawrence Erlbaum Associates, Publishers.

Kane, M. T. (1982). A sampling model for validity. *Applied Psychological Measurement, 6*(2), 125–160.

Kane, M. T. (2006). Validation. In R. L. Brennan (Ed.), *Educational measurement* (4th ed.) (pp. 17–64). Westport, CT: American Council on Education and Praeger Publishers.

Kopriva, R. J. (Ed.) (2008). *Improving testing for English language learners.* New York: Routledge.

Lee, O. (1999). Equity implications based on the conceptions of science achievement in major reform documents. *Review of Educational Research, 69*(1), 83–115.

Martinez, M. E. (1999). Cognition and the question of test item format. *Educational Psychologist, 34*(4), 207–218.

Mazzeo, J., Lazer, S., & Zieky, M. J. (2006). Monitoring educational progress with group-score assessments. In R. L. Brennan (Ed.), *Educational measurement* (4th ed.) (pp. 681–699). Westport, CT: American Council on Education and Praeger Publishers.

National Assessment Governing Board, US Department of Education (2008). *Science assessment and item specifications for the 2009 National Assessment of Educational Progress.* Washington, DC: Author.

National Assessment of Educational Progress (2010). NAEP technical documentation. Retrieved July 1, 2015 from https://nces.ed.gov/nationsreportcard/tdw/analysis/2007/scaling_determination_number_math2007.aspx.

National Research Council (1996). *National science education standards.* National Committee on Science Education Standards and Assessment. Coordinating Council for Education. Washington, DC: National Academy Press.

Pellegrino, J. W., Chudowsky, N., & Glaser, R. (2001). *Knowing what students know: The science and design of educational assessment.* Washington, DC: National Academy Press.

Popham, J. W. (2001). Teaching to the test? *Educational Leadership, 58*(6), 16–20.

Prosser, R. R. & Solano-Flores, G. (2010). *Including English language learners in the process of test development: a study on instrument linguistic adaptation for cognitive validity.* Paper presented at the Annual Conference of the National Council of Measurement in Education, Denver, Colorado, April 29–May 3.

Ruiz-Primo, M. A. & Shavelson, R. J. (1996). Rhetoric and reality in science performance assessment. *Journal of Research in Science Teaching, 33*(10), 1045–1063.

Ruiz-Primo, M. A., Shavelson, R. J., Hamilton, L., & Klein, S. (2002). On the evaluation of systemic science education reform: Searching for instructional sensitivity. *Journal of Research in Science Teaching, 39*(5), 369–393.

Shavelson, R. J. (1995). On the romance of science curriculum and assessment-reform in the United States. In D. K. Sharpes & A. -L. Leino (Eds.), *The dynamic concept of curriculum: Invited papers to honour the memory of Paul Hellgren* (pp. 57–75). Helsinki, Finland: University of Helsinki Department of Education, Research Bulletin 90.

Shepard, L. (2010). What the marketplace has brought us: Item-by-item teaching with little instructional insight. *Peabody Journal of Education, 85,* 246–257.

Sloane, F. C. & Kelly, A. E. (2003). Issues in high-stakes testing programs. *Theory into Practice, 42*(1), 12–17.

Solano-Flores, G. (2000). Teaching and assessing science process skills in physics: The "Bubbles" task. *Science Activities, 37*(1), 31–37.

Solano-Flores, G. & Shavelson, R. J. (1997). Development of performance assessments in science: Conceptual, practical and logistical issues. *Educational Measurement: Issues and Practice, 16*(3), 16–25.

Solano-Flores, G., Trumbull, E., & Nelson-Barber, S. (2002). Concurrent development of dual language assessments: An alternative to translating tests for linguistic minorities. *International Journal of Testing, 2*(2), 107–129.

Thissen-Roe, A., Hunt, E., & Minstrell, J. (2004). The DIAGNOSER project: Combining assessment and learning. *Behavior Research Methods, Instruments & Computers, 36*(2), 234–240.

Trumbull, E. & Solano-Flores, G. (2011). Addressing the language demands of mathematics assessments: Using a language framework and field-based research findings. In M. R. Basterra, E. Trumbull, & G. Solano-Flores (Eds.), *Cultural validity in assessment: Addressing linguistic and cultural diversity* (pp. 218–253). New York: Routledge.

6

FORMATIVE ASSESSMENT

Overview

This chapter discusses formative assessment—assessment that informs instruction. It offers a critical perspective according to which, to effectively support the learning of their ELL students through formative assessment activities, educators need to recognize and address the social dimension of assessment and the fact that assessment activities are mediated by language.

The section "Defining Formative Assessment" discusses current views of formative assessment. The section also discusses the differences between formal and informal formative assessment.

The section "Social Nature of Formative Assessment" discusses how formative assessment is based on social interaction. The ability to take into consideration the social dynamics of team work while conducting formative assessment activities shapes how effectively teachers create opportunities to learn for their ELL students.

The section "Formative Assessment as a Communication Process" provides a perspective according to which assessment involves socialization through language. This perspective, which is useful in the context of large-scale assessment, is especially useful in examining ELL assessment in the classroom context.

The section "Feedback" discusses the challenges of providing effective feedback to ELL students in terms of two dimensions of feedback, quality, and pertinence. Expectations about ELL students and the ability to give them the kind of feedback that is relevant to the learning goals at a given moment influence the effectiveness with which educators support their ELL students' learning through formative assessment.

Defining Formative Assessment

Assessment in the classroom can be thought of as the set of activities performed by teachers with the intent to obtain, process, and interpret information about their students' learning. Assessment is called *formative* when these activities are oriented to obtaining information that allows teachers to adjust their instruction, thus creating opportunities for their students to reach certain learning goals. Referring to formative assessment as assessment *for* learning (as opposed to summative assessment—assessment *of* learning) emphasizes the notion that assessment is also an instructional activity, a set of practices oriented to the construction of learning (Black, 2003).

Formative assessment has been characterized in multiple ways. These different views are not necessarily incompatible—they emphasize different aspects of formative assessment or offer different levels of analysis. For example, Black and Wiliam (1998) identify five basic formative assessment practices: having students know what counts as success, providing feedback to students, questioning activities, self-assessment and peer assessment, and using summative tests formatively. In contrast, Heritage (2007) identifies four elements whose presence is critical to formative assessment: identifying how the students' learning differs from the target state of learning, feedback to teachers and feedback to students, participation of students in assessment activities, and identifying where a given student is in terms of his or her learning in the expected progression towards a learning goal.

Probably the list of formative assessment practices offered by the Qualifications and Curriculum Authority (2003) has the level of specificity that educators need to identify activities that they can recognize or implement in the classroom. According to this list, the teacher:

- performs assessment activities that are embedded in the process of teaching and learning;
- makes learning goals explicit to students;
- helps students to understand and recognize standards to aim for;
- provides feedback that support students to identify the actions they need to take;
- reflects and conveys the commitment for every student to grow;
- engages students in reviewing and reflecting on their own progress; and
- promotes self-assessment among students.

Two forms of formative assessment can be identified—*formal* and *informal*. Table 6.1 compares them as to whether and how the assessment activities are planned, the kind of evidence of learning obtained, and how the teacher interprets or recognizes that evidence and acts on it. Formal formative assessment activities are planned, address content determined by the teacher, produce evidence of learning through conventional assessment procedures (e.g. paper-and-pencil tests),

TABLE 6.1 Characteristics of Formal and Informal Formative Assessment.

Characteristics	Type of Formative Assessment	
	Formal	Informal
Planning and clarifying learning expectations and learning evidence	There is a plan or schedule according to which, at specific points in the curriculum, the teacher collects evidence on their students' learning of specific aspects of content previously identified as relevant to the learning goals.	At any time during instruction, typically without having planned it in advance, the teacher decides to gather or elicit evidence of learning that is critical to meeting the learning goals.
Obtaining evidence of learning	Evidence of learning is collected through activities determined by the teacher according to certain conventions and protocols. All students are required to participate. Students provide information formally, commonly in a non-verbal manner, mostly by answering to specific questions. Typically, students' responses are documented (e.g. in a paper-and-pencil test).	Evidence of learning is gathered, elicited, or encountered through activities that do not follow specific conventions or protocols. These activities may involve the whole class, some students, or individual students. Students' participation (e.g. asking a question or providing an unsolicited answer) may change the direction of instruction. Students provide information casually, both verbally and in a non-verbal manner. Typically, student participation is not documented.
Interpreting or recognizing evidence of learning and using or acting on it	The teacher has time to reflect on the evidence of learning collected and to carefully decide how to act on this evidence (e.g. how to adjust their teaching and the characteristics of the comments and feedback they intend to give to students).	The teacher needs to act immediately on the evidence of learning gathered, elicited, or encountered. This takes place spontaneously and in multiple possible ways (e.g. by repeating information, conducting a demonstration, or answering with a question).

involve the entire class, and take place in ways that allow the teacher to reflect on the information collected to make instructional decisions.

In contrast, informal formative assessment is typically not planned; the teacher takes actions oriented to producing evidence of learning as it is needed (e.g. asking students to raise their hands if they understand an explanation) or reacts to situations that arise during instruction (e.g. answering a question asked by a student). In addition, in informal formative assessment, not all students necessarily participate in these activities and their participation is not scripted.

While authors recognize that knowledge is constructed in a sociocultural context and assessment activities involve both teachers and students (e.g. Brookhart, 2007; Moss, 2008; Shepard, 2000), literature on formative assessment is yet to address linguistic diversity in the classroom systematically. With few exceptions (e.g. Abedi, 2010; Del Rosal, 2015; Ruiz-Primo, Solano-Flores, & Li, 2014), little has been said about ELL students in the context of formative assessment.

Social Nature of Formative Assessment

Formative Assessment as a Social Process

Formative assessment can be viewed as a process in which teachers and students engage during instruction (Linquanti, 2014). Viewing this process as a social process is particularly important in the linguistically diverse classroom. Ruiz-Primo and Li (2012) offer a conceptual framework of formative assessment that includes social participation (Figure 6.1). Critical to effective formative assessment is the extent to which activities address the classroom context in which it is circumscribed. In accordance with Sadler (1989) and Bell and Cowie (2001), the framework identifies four types of activities: (A) clarifying learning expectations (goals), (B) collecting information, (C) interpreting information, and (D) acting on/using the information collected towards the learning goals. These four activities define a formative assessment event.

While formative assessment events can be completed in multiple ways (e.g. through classroom conversations, peer assessment, or the use of quizzes), they need to be completed in a cyclical sequence if they are to be effective. For example, a substantial improvement of instruction will not take place if the teacher fails to properly adjust instruction according to information collected and interpreted in Activities A, B, and C (Ruiz-Primo & Furtak, 2007).

Each of the activities in the formative assessment cycle involves certain teaching practices and requires the social participation of students. To be effective, formative assessment cannot be exclusively under the teacher's control. For example, it needs to encourage students to ask questions, give opinions, or express agreement or disagreement. It is through social participation that students become actors in the classroom, in the sense that they take responsibility of their own learning through the development of self-assessment and metacognitive skills.

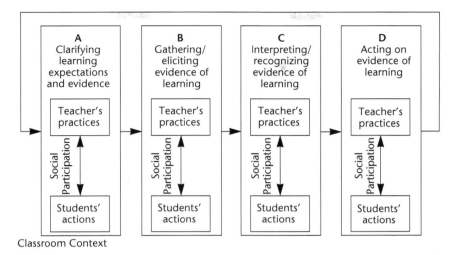

Classroom Context

FIGURE 6.1   Formative assessment as a process that takes place through social interaction. Based on Ruiz-Primo & Li (2012).

Social Structure

The notion of inclusion—efforts to ensure access to a wide variety of opportunities to learn for all students (see Kozleski, Artiles, Fletcher, & Engelbrecht, 2009)—and Bourdieu's (1984, 2003) ideas concerning social reproduction help to understand the role of educators as facilitators of social interaction during the implementation of formative assessment activities. Without proper guidance from teachers, patterns in the roles adopted by the students or assigned to them in formative assessment activities may reproduce social inequalities and produce an unequal distribution of opportunities to learn.

Suppose that a teacher has the students break up into small teams of three persons each to discuss a topic in the social sciences class and take a position concerning a dilemma. Each team member has to perform one of three activities: taking notes, organizing materials, and reporting the team's conclusions to the rest of the class.

It should not be assumed that this activity will give the same set of opportunities to all students without careful guidance. This is especially the case for ELL students, some of which may find it within their area of comfort to remain silent during the team's discussions and take roles that involve limited social interaction and limited use of language. A given ELL student may consistently avoid being the reporter. Another ELL student may attempt to have a more active participation, but the other team members may overpower her during discussions limiting the opportunities for her to express her ideas, or may pay little attention to her when she speaks.

Concerned that difficulty communicating in English might be a source of frustration for ELL students or an obstacle to completing the assigned tasks, teachers may consistently have them work in teams only with other ELL students. While well intentioned, this approach may isolate ELL students socially because it strips them from opportunities to exchange ideas with other students and to interact with native English speakers in ways that support their development of English.

Clearly, because social interaction is critical to the successful completion of formative assessment activities, educators need to be mindful about the ways in which students interact and need to be active in promoting equitable peer interaction. Through proper classroom management, educators can ensure that each ELL student is given a voice in group activities, interacts with each of the other students in the class, and has the opportunity to play multiple roles throughout the school year. Using Rogoff's (1995) ideas of social participation, it can be said that educators need to make an effort to continuously support each ELL student in moving from novice to apprentice and from apprentice to actor—a plane of social participation in which the student appropriates classroom's social practices.

Student Interaction and Code-Switching

As any other bilinguals in the world, ELLs may switch between languages during conversation, especially while they work together in small teams. Fearing that code-switching may hamper development of English, teachers may decide not to allow their ELL students to use their first language in classroom activities. As discussed in Chapter 2, these concerns have no solid grounds. Using their first language does not prevent emergent bilinguals from developing a second language.

ELL students engaged in an activity involving team work are likely to code-switch because they are using the linguistic resources they have in their two languages to construct knowledge collaboratively. For example, while solving a mathematical problem, two ELL students may use English or their first language depending on which language they feel serves better a specific communication function (e.g. argumentation, disagreement). Thus, in making an argument, a girl uses her first language to express disagreement and try to change her peer's mind regarding the approach being used to solve a problem. Yet she resorts to English to use the mathematical terms that she has learned in English at school (Moschkovich, 2007).

As the example shows, code-switching is a natural behavior. Preventing ELL students from using their two languages hampers their ability to construct knowledge through social interaction.

Formative Assessment as a Communication Process

As discussed in Chapter 2, assessment can be characterized as a communication process. Even in the context of large-scale assessment, in which students are unknown to the creators of tests, assessment can be described as a process (Solano-Flores, 2008) in which the assessment system asks questions (the test items), students respond to those questions, and the assessment system reacts to those questions (e.g. by assigning scores to those responses).

In the classroom context, the nature of formative assessment as a communication process is more evident (Ruiz-Primo, 2011; Ruiz-Primo, Solano-Flores, & Li, 2014). The formative assessment cycle necessarily takes place through teacher–student interaction mediated by language. Thus, successful completion of formative assessment activities may be a challenge for both ELL students and their teachers if teachers do not address language issues effectively. Especially important in formative assessment practices for ELL students are teachers' perceptions of students' English proficiency, the effective use of multiple semiotic resources, the use of appropriate wait times during instruction, and the fair sampling of students.

Educators' Perceptions of Students' English Proficiency

A potential, undesired misuse of English proficiency tests may occur when educators' perceptions of ELL students' communication skills are based solely on the limited number of English proficiency categories into which ELL students are classified. For example, the label "Limited English Proficient" may create in the educator the wrong perception of ELL students as individuals who are incapable of communicating in English in any way. This is especially the case when teachers are not provided with detailed information of their ELL students' skills in English, or when that information is difficult to interpret.

As seen in Chapter 4, the majority of ELL students have a minimum level of command of English that allows them to interact with other students and with their teachers. Thus, teachers should not feel intimidated by the fact that they do not speak their ELL students' language. It is important for them to talk to ELL students all the time, even if these students may not understand everything that is said to them in English. The strategy parallels the natural behavior parents have with their children—they speak to them from the time they are born, rather than waiting for them to be fully proficient in their language. Talking to their ELL students and interacting with them allows teachers to develop a sense of each student's skills in English and devise effective instructional strategies in support of students' individual needs.

Semiotic Resources

Meaning can be conveyed using multiple forms of representation (Lemke, 1998). Classroom interaction takes place through different semiotic modes, for example orally (e.g. in classroom conversations), through text, graphically (e.g. using drawings, maps, tables), and through non-verbal forms of communication (e.g. gestures, facial expressions, pointing at objects). It also takes place through the use of different means of communication such as books, handouts, projector slides, posters, or the Internet. The term *semiotic resources* is used to refer to the multiple forms in which information can be represented and communicated (Kress, 2010).

While teachers intuitively use multiple semiotic resources in their teaching all the time, this practice can be enacted more deliberately and systematically in their formative assessment activities to ensure the participation of their ELL students. This practice should involve both teachers and students. For example, in clarifying the learning goals of an activity, the teacher may explain verbally to the whole class how those goals are related to activities performed before. As she speaks, the teacher writes on the board key concepts or new or difficult words, and points at posters and realia to support her explanation. When she collects information about their learning, the teacher invites her students to ask questions or ask the whole class to show thumbs up to indicate understanding.

The participation of ELL students in formative assessment activities can be facilitated by providing an environment in which they feel comfortable using multiple semiotic resources in combination. Directions such as *show me with your hands* and *draw here on the board to help you explain* are examples that illustrate how students can be invited to use multiple semiotic resources to communicate.

It is important to keep in mind that semiotic resources should not be assumed to be exchangeable. While the same information can be represented in multiple forms, each semiotic resource has a unique set of affordances and limitations. As an example, think about explaining the process of growth of a plant over time verbally, by drawing a graph, and by moving the hand in a way that mimics the shape of the line of that graph. These resources vary on the level of detail with which they represent information. Also, they vary on how effectively they communicate that information to different students depending on their proficiency in English and their familiarity with graphs and the kinds of gestures used by the teacher.

Using several semiotic resources in combination in formative assessment activities promotes the participation of ELL students and supports them to navigate across multiple forms of representation. However, while they should be used in combination, different semiotic resources should not be assumed to be exchangeable. For example, sometimes pictures and images are wrongly thought to be "worth a thousand words." Such misconceptions may lead educators to assume that ELL students should always be asked to respond to questions on written tests by making drawings, or to assume that any direction given to ELL students should depend totally on pictorial representations of information.

Wait Time

Wait time appears to play an important role in the ways in which ELL students can benefit from informal formative assessment. *Wait time* is the average lapse between utterances in teacher–student one-on-one interactions (Rowe, 1974). A large body of literature documents that, typically (Figure 6.2a), teachers wait an

(a) Typical Wait Times

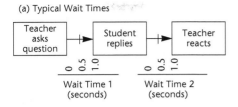

(b) Enhanced Wait Times

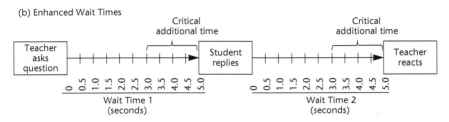

FIGURE 6.2 Teacher-student interactions and the average length of pauses after the teacher asks a question to a student (Wait Time 1) and after the student replies (Wait Time 2): (a) Interactions with typical wait times; (b) Interactions with enhanced wait times.

average of roughly one second for a student to respond to a question (Wait Time 1) and roughly one second to react after the student responds to a question (e.g. by asking another question to the student, asking the same question to another student, or moving on with their teaching) (Wait Time 2).

This average wait time length of one second observed in teaching appears to follow the typical turn-taking silence gap patterns in everyday life conversation (see Heldner & Edlund, 2010). In the context of instruction, the time between turns in conversation needs to be longer to produce effective interactions. Quick teacher reactions appear to limit students' opportunities to elaborate their responses and do not allow teachers to give careful consideration of their students' responses.

A wealth of evidence shows that simply increasing Wait Time 1 and Wait Time 2 (Figure 6.2b) contributes to improving the frequency and quality of student participation in class (e.g. Sadker *et al.*, 2007), the performance of students in tests (Tobin, 1980), and the quality of teacher and student discourse (Tobin, 1986). For example, increases in the frequency and length of the students' responses and the frequency of unsolicited and correct responses are observed when teachers increase their wait time to three to five seconds (Rowe, 1986). There is evidence that the frequency and quality of the participation of cultural minority students who have been previously identified as non-verbal increase when the average wait time is increased systematically (see Rowe, 1986).

White male students tend to receive longer wait times than female students and students of color—a fact that has been argued to be a reflection of cultural stereotypes and the sets of expectations teachers have about their students (see Sadker *et al.*, 2007). This evidence speaks to the importance of teachers' expectations of their students in formative assessment. Driven by overly simple perceptions of their ELL students' ability to communicate in English, some teachers may give shorter wait times to ELL students than other students, thus giving ELL students fewer opportunities to think, give answers, or elaborate their ideas. A factor contributing to this trend is the differences in communication styles of different cultural groups. As discussed in Chapter 3, different cultures encourage among their children different ways of asking questions to and responding to questions from adults. In some cultures, responding quickly to an adult's question without seeming to think carefully about it might be considered impolite (Kusimo *et al.*, 2000). Being aware of these factors should help teachers to implement formative assessment for their ELL students more effectively.

Sampling

As defined in Chapter 1, *sampling* is the activity consisting of selecting and examining the portion of a whole with the intent to make generalizations about the whole based on the characteristics of that portion, called *sample*. Sampling is necessary in many cases because, due to practical limitations, it is impossible to examine a population in its entirety.

The notion of sampling comes handy in the context of formative assessment for ELL students because, due to time constraints, it is not always possible to collect information on each student's learning (Ruiz-Primo, 2013). At least intuitively, teachers perform sampling routinely to obtain accurate information about the progress of their classes towards the learning goals. For example, based on a few questions he asks of three or four students, a teacher gauges how far or close the whole class is from meeting certain learning goals and decides how he needs to adjust his teaching to meet those learning goals.

If this teacher has the tendency to obtain that information more frequently from his most active, participating students, or only from non-ELL students, then his samples of students will be biased because these samples will systematically include some students and exclude others. These biased samples are likely to mislead his instructional decisions in the sense that the ways in which he adjusts his teaching will not work to the benefit of all his students.

As an effort oriented to ensuring that their formative assessment activities are completed successfully, teachers can reflect continuously on the ways in which they interact with their students. Using a sampling perspective, they can use the indicators shown in Table 6.2 to reflect on effective sampling and the inclusiveness of their formative assessment activities. The list is not exhaustive but gives an idea of the multiple ways in which the notion of sampling can be used to ensure inclusive assessment formative assessment.

TABLE 6.2 Indicators of Effective Sampling in Formative Assessment Practices.

1. ELLs are proportionately represented in the samples of students from which the teacher obtains information to determine where the class is with respect to the learning goals.
2. The proportion of ELL students who participate during an activity reflects the proportion of ELL and non-ELL students in the class.
3. When talking to the whole class, the teacher makes eye contact with ELL and non-ELL students with the same frequency.
4. The teacher calls on ELL students to encourage their participation when these students are not participating.
5. The proportion of ELL students who are asked questions individually during an activity reflects the proportion of ELL and non-ELL students in the class.
6. Average wait times in one-on-one conversations are the same for ELL and non-ELL students.

Feedback

Feedback deserves special consideration as a relevant aspect of formative assessment for ELL students. In the context of instruction, *feedback* has been defined as "information provided by an agent (e.g., teacher, peer, book, parent, self, experience) regarding aspects of one's performance or understanding" (Hattie & Timperley, 2007, p. 81). While authors vary in the characteristics that define effective feedback, there is agreement that such characteristics include a high level of explicitness of the information provided to students on where they are with respect to a learning goal (Furtak, 2009).

Recent conceptual developments provide a perspective according to which feedback should be viewed as a complex process guided by a learning goal that actively involves students. This process should be regarded as an instructional scaffold intended to improve learning outcomes and processes (e.g. metacognition). Feedback should be accessible and practical, should be aligned with a learning trajectory, and should consider multiple sources of information about the students' learning (Ruiz-Primo & Li, 2013).

Building on these ideas, two aspects of feedback can be identified as especially important in formative assessment practices concerning ELL students: quality and pertinence.

Feedback Quality

There is evidence that links student academic achievement with the quality of feedback received during instruction (Black & Wiliam, 1998). Also, there is evidence that low levels of communication skills and understanding, as reflected by the characteristics of the information written by students in their science notebooks, might be due to a large extent to the absence of feedback from teachers (Ruiz-Primo, 2004).

As with other aspects of formative assessment, research on feedback is practically silent about ELL students. However, there is evidence that the kind of information provided by teachers reacting to their students' work tends to be different for ELL and non-ELL students. Initial findings from a project that examined multiple lessons in culturally diverse classrooms indicate that teachers do not spend the same time providing feedback to their ELL and non-ELL students (Note 6.1).

Table 6.3 shows the frequency of different types of information provided by teachers in an investigation that examined how teachers reacted to different forms of work from their ELL and non-ELL students (Zhao, Solano-Flores, & Qian, 2015). The table shows data for two forms of student work: quiz and exit ticket (Note 6.2). The information provided by teachers is presented in four categories, ordered from the top to the bottom in ascending level of explicitness—level of detail. Thus, "Comments" is the most sophisticated type of information provided to students and the closest category to what can be considered as high quality feedback—although it is important to mention that the coding did not consider the content of the comments.

Consistent with findings that teachers tended to focus on grading (see Mehan, 2008), a grade was the type of information teachers provided to students more frequently. Teachers gave grades to quizzes from ELL students and non-ELL students with the same frequency but gave grades to exit tickets more frequently to ELL students than non-ELL students. In contrast, teachers provided comments on quizzes more frequently to non-ELL students than ELL students. Clearly, teachers missed valuable opportunities to provide effective feedback to all their students, especially for their ELL students. This finding speaks to the need for educators to make a deliberate, systematic effort to provide elaborated comments to all students on their work.

TABLE 6.3 Type of Information Provided by Teachers on Different Forms of Student Work: Percentage of Student Products (Rounded). Based on Zhao, Solano-Flores and Qian (2015).

	Non-ELL		ELL	
Type of Information	*Quiz (n = 27)*	*Exit Ticket (n = 24)*	*Quiz (n = 28)*	*Exit Ticket (n = 17)*
Grade	100	58	100	76
Evaluative symbols (e.g. check marks)	74	58	79	24
Highlighting (e.g. circling a sentence)	33	4	25	6
Comments	67	8	46	0

Feedback Pertinence

An important aspect of formative assessment concerns the relevance of the feedback educators give to their ELL students. Research on college tutoring shows that expert tutors ignore their students' errors when those errors are not relevant to successfully completing the activities at hand (Lepper, Drake, & O'Donnell-Johnson, 1997). These lessons help educators to reason about the kind of feedback they need to give to their ELL students under a given set of circumstances and given a certain set of learning goals.

Suppose that, during the science class, the teacher asks a pair of students to report on the experiment they are conducting. One of them, an ELL student, responds:

> –Michael and me were trying...
> (The teacher interrupts:)
> –It's "Michael and I," not "Michael and me."
> (The student continues:)
> –OK.... Michael and I were trying to put water in the bottle...
> (The teacher interrupts again:)
> –FLASK.... "We were trying to FILL the FLASK with water."
> (The student continues:)
> –Yes. Fill the flask with water. But the thing was more big.
> (The teacher interrupts again:)
> –You mean, "BIGGER"...

The teacher certainly provides feedback. But that feedback is not relevant to the science learning goal beyond formal aspects of communication. By focusing on these formal aspects, the attention is diverted away from the science activity being discussed. By the time he finishes reporting on the experiment, the student will probably be too frustrated to benefit from any feedback on the science content.

This is not to say that ELLs should not be supported in developing their second language, for example by rephrasing what they say. Yet educators have to be mindful about timing and the kind of feedback that is likely to be effective, given the learning goals at a given moment. Properly supporting ELL students require viewing these students not only as English language learners but also, and above all, as learners.

Closing Comments

The perspective of assessment as a process of social interaction through language plays a critical role in the implementation of formal assessment activities, especially for ELL students. Viewing formative assessment as a communication process enables teachers to appreciate the importance of obtaining information about the progress of *all* their students if they are to make sound instructional decisions.

This communication perspective also allows educators to evaluate the extent to which ELL students and their non-ELL peers are given the same opportunities to learn through assessment activities in the classroom. Equal representation of ELLs in all classroom activities and a deliberate, systematic effort to provide equal opportunities to all students are critical to attaining high quality formative assessment for ELL students.

Exercises

Exercise 6.1: Classroom Context and Formative Assessment

1. A school district is interested in purchasing packages of interim assessments for each grade and each content area. The packages are to be distributed to teachers for them to administer to their students every six weeks to inform their instruction, thus standardizing formative assessment activities across classrooms. Before making a decision, the district would like to have your opinion. Do you think that purchasing packages of interim assessment activities for teachers is a good idea? Make a recommendation and justify your answer based on what you know have learned about formative assessment.

Exercise 6.2: Feedback

1. Describe an instance in which you provided feedback to your students as part of your teaching.
2. Discuss whether and how the feedback you provided had each of the qualities of effective feedback listed below:
   - Timely (immediate)
   - Specific (identifies what needs to be improved and why)
   - Constructive (provides actions and strategies for improvement)
   - Focused on actions or outcomes (not persons)
   - Verified (ensures student understands the feedback)
3. Discuss any actions you think you should take to ensure that you provide more feedback than grades on the students' work.
4. Discuss any actions you think you should take to ensure that your ELL students receive from you the same quality of feedback you give to your non-ELL students.

Exercise 6.3: Social Interaction and Formative Assessment

1. Keep a log of the sampling strategies you use as part of your informal formative assessment activities. Every day for ten days, using the format shown in Figure 6.3, describe the actions you take to ensure proper sampling in the

way you implement informal formative assessment for each of the six criteria listed. The actions you describe may be from different activities or different classes.

2. Include in your log information on the circumstances under which you take the actions described, your thoughts, and the challenges you face in ensuring proper sampling. When you do not have actions to report for a given criterion, explain the reasons that prevented you from meeting that criterion.

3. When you complete your log, examine how your sampling strategies have changed. Also discuss how any changes in your practice have contributed to improving your informal formative assessment skills.

4. Discuss whether and how your efforts to ensuring proper sampling in your informal formative assessment practices has had any effect on your ELL students.

Date: _____

Criterion	*Example*
• ELLs are proportionately represented in the samples of students from which the teacher collects information to determine where the class is with respect to the learning goals.	
• The proportion of ELL students who participate during an activity reflects the proportion of ELL and non-ELL students in the class.	
• When talking to the whole class, the teacher makes eye contact with ELL and non-ELL students with the same frequency.	
• The teacher calls on ELL students to encourage their participation when these students are not participating.	
• The proportion of ELL students who are asked questions individually during an activity reflects the proportion of ELL and non-ELL students in the class.	
• Average wait times in one-on-one conversations are the same for ELL and non-ELL students.	

FIGURE 6.3 Format for reporting sampling strategies.

Exercise 6.4: Social Interaction and Formative Assessment

`1. Ruiz-Primo & Furtak (2007) offer the ESRU cycle, a model for describing the cyclical nature of interactions in informal formative assessment activities. The ESRU cycle consists of four steps:

E. the teacher **e**licits a response;

S. the **s**tudents respond;

R. the teacher **r**ecognizes critical information from the students' responses;

U. the teacher **u**ses the information collected and takes actions to support the students' learning

The elements of this cycle take place naturally in classroom conversations. However, the cycle is not always completed. There is evidence that links the student academic achievement with their teachers' ability to complete the ESRU cycle in their classroom conversations.

2. Using the format shown in Figure 6.4, report on five ESRU cycles you are able to complete. The cycles reported should come from different days. For each ESRU cycle, provide, in the box, *Context*, information on the context

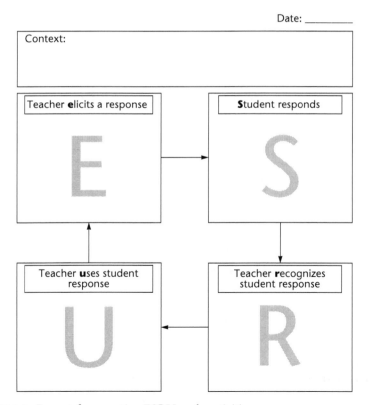

FIGURE 6.4 Format for reporting ESRU cycle activities.

in which the cycle occurs (e.g. the learning goals, the conversation within which the cycle initiates, the topic being discussed). Then, in the appropriate box, provide the details corresponding to each of the four steps (e.g. in the E box, describe the actions you take or the questions ask to elicit a response). Make sure you report how, in the ESRU cycles, you pay attention to the needs of your ELL students.

3. Make sure you fill out your ESRU cycle reports as soon as possible after they take place, so that you do not forget important details.
4. Once you have your five reports, discuss how easy or difficult it was for you to complete the ESRU cycles.
5. Discuss the challenges you faced when you attempted to include ELL students in the ESRU cycles.
6. Discuss what you have learned from this experience about your formative assessment practices in general and with regard to your ELL students, in particular.

Notes

Note 6.1. The findings are from a National Science Foundation–funded project, currently in progress: Solano-Flores, G., Ruiz-Primo, M. A., & Li, M. (2011). Collaborative research: *Examining formative assessment practices for English language learners in science classrooms*. National Science Foundation project, DRK-12 Program DRL-1118844.

Note 6.2. *Quiz* was defined as a brief paper-and-pencil test. *Exit ticket* was defined as a format in which students reported the activities they performed and the content they learned during a lesson.

References

Abedi, J. (2010). Research and recommendations for formative assessment with ELLs. In H. L. Andrade & G. J. Cizek (Eds.), *Handbook of formative assessment* (pp. 181–197). New York: Routledge.

Bell, B. & Cowie, B. (2001). *Formative assessment and science education*. Dordrecht, The Netherlands: Kluwer Academic Publishers.

Black, P. (2003). The importance of everyday assessment. In J. M. Atkin & J. E. Coffey (Eds.), *Everyday assessment in the classroom*. Arlington, VA: NSTA Press. (pp. 1–11).

Black, P. & Wiliam, D. (1998). Assessment and classroom learning. *Assessment in Education*, 5(1), 7–74.

Bourdieu, P. (1984). Distinction: A social critique of the judgment of taste. Cambridge, MA: Harvard University Press.

Bourdieu, P. (2003). *Language & symbolic power*. Cambridge, MA: Harvard University Press (Original work published in 1977).

Brookhart, S. M. (2007). Expanding views about formative classroom assessment: A review of the literature. In J. H. McMillan (Ed.), *Formative classroom assessment: Theory into practice* (pp. 43–62). New York: Teacher College Press.

Del Rosal, K. (2015). *Investigating informal formative assessment practices addressing emergent bilinguals' science academic language.* Doctoral dissertation. University of Colorado Boulder.

Furtak, E. M. (2009). *Formative assessment for secondary science teachers.* Thousand Oaks, CA: Corwin.

Hattie, J. & Timperley, H. (2007). The power of feedback. *Review of Educational Research,* 77(1), 81–82.

Heldner, M. & Edlund, J. (2010). Pauses, gaps and overlaps in conversations. *Journal of Phonetics, 38,* 555–568.

Heritage, M. (2007). Formative assessment: What do teachers need to know and do? *Phi Delta Kappan, 89*(2), 140–145.

Kozleski, E. B., Artiles, A. J., Fletcher, T., & Engelbrecht, P. (2009). Understanding the dialectics of the local and the global in Education for All: A comparative case study. *International Critical Childhood Policy Studies Journal, 2*(1), 15–29.

Kress, G. (2010). *Mutimodality: A social semiotic approach to contemporary communication.* New York: Routledge.

Kusimo, P., Ritter, M. G., Busick, K., Ferguson, C., Trumbull, E., & Solano-Flores, G. (2000). *Making assessment work for everyone: How to build on student strengths.* Regional Educational Laboratories. Retrieved September 17, 2014 from http://www.sedl.org/pubs/tl05/.

Lemke, J. L. (1998). Multiplying meaning: Visual and verbal semiotics in scientific text. In J. R. Martin & R. Veel (Eds.), *Reading science: Critical and functional perspectives on discourses of science* (pp. 87–113). New York: Routledge.

Lepper, M. R., Drake, M. F., & O'Donnell-Johnson, T. (1997). Scaffolding techniques of expert human tutors. In K. Hogan & M. Pressley (Eds.), *Scaffolding student learning: Instructional approaches & issues* (pp. 108–144). Cambridge, MA: Brookline Books.

Linquanti, R. (2012). *Supporting formative assessment for deeper learning: A primer for policymakers.* Washington, DC: Council of Chief State School Officers.

Mehan, H. (2008). A sociocultural perspective on opportunity to learn and assessment. In P. A. Moss, D. Pullin, J. P. Gee, E. H. Haertel, & L. J. Young (Eds.), *Assessment, equity, and opportunity to learn* (pp. 42–75). New York: Cambridge University Press.

Moschkovich, J. N. (2007). Using two languages while learning mathematics. *Educational Studies in Mathematics, 64*(2), 121–144.

Moss, P. A. (2008). Sociocultural implications for the practice of assessment I: Classroom assessment. In P. A. Moss, D. Pullin, J. P. Gee, E. H. Haertel, & L. J. Young, (Eds.), *Assessment, equity, and opportunity to learn.* New York: Cambridge University Press.

Qualifications and Curriculum Authority (QCA)(2003). Assessment for Learning. Retrieved June 16, 2005 from http://www.qca.org.uk/ca/5-14/afl/.

Rogoff, B. (1995). Observing sociocultural activity on three planes: Participatory appropriation, guided participation, and apprenticeship. In J. V. Wertsch, P. del Río, & A. Alvarez (Eds.), *Sociocultural studies of mind*. New York: Cambridge University Press.

Rowe, M. B. (1974). Wait-time and rewards as instructional variables, their influence on language, logic, and fate control: Part one-wait-time. *Journal of Research in Science Teaching, 11*(2), 81–84.

Rowe, M. B. (1986). Wait time: Slowing down may be a way of speeding up! *Journal of Teacher Education, 37*, 43–48.

Ruiz-Primo, M. A. & Li, M. (2012). Examining formative feedback in the classroom context: New research perspectives. In J. H. McMillan (Ed.), *Handbook of research on classroom assessment* (pp. 215–232). Los Angeles: SAGE Publications.

Ruiz-Primo, M. A. (2004). Evaluating students' science notebooks as an assessment tool. *International Journal of Science Education, 26*(2), 1477–1506.

Ruiz-Primo, M. A. (2011) Informal formative assessment: The role of instructional dialogues in assessing students' learning. *Studies of Educational Evaluation, 37*(1), 15–24.

Ruiz-Primo, M. A. (2013, April). Formative assessment in multilingual classrooms. Keynote address. *Center for Culturally Responsive Evaluation and Assessment Inaugural Conference*. Chicago: University of Illinois at Urbana–Champaign.

Ruiz-Primo, M. A. & Furtak, E. M. (2007). Exploring teachers' informal formative assessment practices and students' understanding in the context of scientific inquiry. *Journal of Research in Science Teaching, 44*(1), 57–84.

Ruiz-Primo, M. A. & Li, M. (2013). Examining formative feedback in the classroom context: New research perspectives. In J. H. McMillan (Ed.), *Handbook of research on classroom assessment* (pp. 215–232). Los Angeles: Sage.

Ruiz-Primo, M. A., Solano-Flores, G., & Li, M. (2014). Formative assessment as a process of interaction through language: A framework for the inclusion of English language learners. In C. Wyatt-Smith, V. Klenowski, & P. Colbert, (Ed.), *Developing assessment for quality learning: The enabling power of assessment, Vol 1.* (pp. 265–282). Dordrecht: Springer.

Sadker, D., Zittleman, K., Earley, P., McCormick, T., Strawn, C., & Preston, J. (2007). The treatment of gender equity in teacher education, In S. S. Klein, B. Richardson, D. A. Grayson, L. H. Fox, C. Kramarae, D. Pollard, & C. A. Dwyer (Eds.), *Handbook for achieving gender equity through education* (2nd ed.). Mahwah, NJ: Lawrence Erlbaum Associates.

Sadler, D. R. (1989). Formative assessment in the design of instructional assessments. *Instructional Science, 18*, 119–144.

Shepard, L. A. (2000). The role of assessment in a learning culture. *Educational Researcher, 29*(7), 4–14.

Solano-Flores, G. (2008). Who is given tests in what language by whom, when, and where? The need for probabilistic views of language in the testing of English language learners. *Educational Researcher, 37*(4), 189–199.

Solano-Flores, G., Ruiz-Primo, M. A., & Li, M. (2011). Collaborative research: Examining formative assessment practices for English language learners in science classrooms. National Science Foundation project, DRK-12 Program DRL-1118844.

Tobin, K. (1980). The effect of an extended teacher wait-time on science achievement. *Journal of Research in Science Teaching, 17*(5), 469–475.

Tobin, K. (1986). Effects of teacher wait time on discourse characteristics in mathematics and language arts classes. *American Educational Research Journal, 23*(2), 191–200.

Zhao, X., Solano-Flores, G., & Qian, M. (2015). *Examining teachers' feedback for English language learners in science classrooms.* Paper presented at the Annual Meeting of the American Educational Research Association. Chicago, April 16–20.

7

ACCOMMODATIONS AND ACCESSIBILITY RESOURCES

Overview

This chapter discusses the possibilities and limitations of *test taking support devices*, a term used here to refer to both testing accommodations and accessibility resources in the testing of ELL students. These support devices are intended to minimize the effects of limited proficiency in the language of testing as an extraneous factor that adversely affects the performance of ELL students on tests.

Educators are often in charge of providing testing accommodations authorized by large-scale assessment systems or deciding the kinds of accessibility resources that are to be made available to a given student during testing. Being aware of the limitations and possibilities of these test taking support devices helps them to make appropriate decisions on their use.

The section "Characteristics of Test Taking Support Devices" provides definitions of testing accommodations and accessibility resources. The difference between testing accommodations and accessibility resources is not always clear. For the purposes of this book, the distinction is based on the extent to which they are sensitive to the needs of students and, more specifically, to the extent to which they are capable of reacting to the students' actions.

The section "Effectiveness of Testing Accommodation" provides a critical perspective of results from research on accommodations for ELL students. The section discusses the limitations of accommodations in their effectiveness to reduce the score gap between ELL and non-ELL students that is attributable to English proficiency and the reasons that account for those limitations. The section also discusses limitations of current assessment policies concerning the use of testing accommodations with ELL students.

The section "Increasing the Effectiveness of Test Taking Support Devices" discusses deterministic and probabilistic approaches that guide the actions of researchers and decision makers in their attempts to maximize the effectiveness of test taking support devices.

The section "Selecting and Using Test Taking Support Devices" offers a set of five criteria for thinking critically about the possibilities and limitations of test taking support devices. These criteria are also intended to help educators to have realistic expectations about what test taking support devices can do in support of their ELL students.

The notion of accessibility resource is becoming increasingly meaningful as information technology makes it possible to customize the interface used to the test students with computers. Due to the relative recency of this trend, more literature is available on the effectiveness of testing accommodations than it is on the effectiveness of accessibility resources. As a consequence, some of the issues discussed for testing accommodations are not discussed for accessibility resources.

Characteristics of Test Taking Support Devices

Testing Accommodations

The term *testing accommodations* refers to modifications of the characteristics of tests or the ways in which they are administered. These modifications are intended to remove the effects of limited proficiency in the language in which tests are administered as an extraneous factor that influence the performance of ELL students on those tests. These modifications should not give and unfair advantage of ELL over other students (Abedi, Lord, Hofstetter, & Baker, 2001). Testing accommodations can also be defined as modifications of tests intended to ensure that ELL students gain access to the content of items. *Gaining access* means being able to understand the content of items, what they ask, and what examinees are supposed to do to provide their responses.

Typically, accommodations are provided in a blanket manner. That means that a given accommodation is provided exactly in the same way to all recipient students. Testing students with tests in their native language, reading aloud for them the directions of tests in English, simplifying the text of the items with the intent to reduce their reading demands, and giving students additional time to complete their tests are among the many forms of accommodations used by different state assessment systems in the US. The spectrum of testing accommodations is wide (see Sireci, Li, & Scarpati, 2003). Practically every assessment program authorizes the use of one or several forms of accommodations intended to ensure ELL students' access to the content of items. Table 7.1 shows some of the 44 accommodations that Rivera and Collum (2004) reported in a study that examined the different accommodations used by states to test ELL students in large-scale assessment programs.

TABLE 7.1 Some Accommodations Cited in States' Assessment Policies. Adapted from Rivera and Collum (2004, 2006).

Direct Linguistic Support		*Indirect Linguist Support*
In Students' First Language	*In English*	
Written Translation	**Simplification**	**Test Schedule**
• Written directions	• Simplified directions	• Extra test time
• Side-by-side bilingual format	• Test items read aloud in simplified English	• Subtests flexibly scheduled
• Translated test in first language	• Linguistically simplified test	• Test administered at time of day most
Scripted Oral Translation	**Multiple Sensory Modalities**	beneficial to student
• Oral translation of directions	• Directions read aloud in English	• Continuous breaks during test sessions
• Audio-recorded directions in first language	• Directions repeated in English	**Testing Conditions**
• Audio-recorded test items in first language	• Audio-recorded directions in English	• Test administered individually
Sight Translation	• Oral and written directions in English	• Test administered in small group
• Directions translated into first language	• Key words and phrases in directions highlighted	• Teacher faces student
• Directions explained/ clarified in first language	• Key words and phrases in test highlighted	• Test administered in location with minimal distraction
• Test items read aloud in first language	• Test items read aloud in English	• Student-provided preferential seating
• Interpreter provided	• Audio-recorded items in English	• Student takes test in separate location
Student Response	**Clarification/ Verification**	• Test administered by bilingual teacher
• Student responds in first language	• Directions clarified	• Test administered in ESL/bilingual classroom
	• Words on test defined or explained	• Test administered in room familiar to
	• Spelling support with dictionaries or spell/ grammar checkers	student

Note: The list does not include all the accommodations reported in the original documents.

Accessibility Resources

The term *accessibility resources* is used to refer to the means made available for students to use as they need them to overcome linguistic challenges of items that are not related to the content being assessed (see Chía, 2015; Solano-Flores, Shade, & Chrzanowski, 2014). Unlike testing accommodations, which are fixed in the sense that they are intended to be provided in the same way to all examinees, accessibility resources are sensitive at least to some extent to the specific needs of each individual student. For example, the translation of a test is the same for all students who receive this accommodation. In contrast, a dictionary with definitions or translations of words alphabetically ordered can be used, at least in principle, by each student as needed (Note 7.1).

Thanks to the information technology used to administer tests by computer in large-scale testing programs, it is possible to support ELL students through more sophisticated accessibility resources that react to the students' actions (see Abedi, 2014; Chía, 2015; Measured Progress & National Center on Educational Outcomes, 2014; Measured Progress & ETS Collaborative, 2012). For example, an item displayed on the screen of the computer shows some words or terms highlighted, indicating that translations for those terms are available. When the student clicks on one of those highlighted terms, a pop-up window appears showing its translation (Smarter Balanced Assessment Consortium, 2014). Through interaction with the computer, the student uses the translation support as needed.

Effectiveness of Testing Accommodations

Evidence of Effectiveness

Research on the effectiveness of testing accommodations has focused mainly on providing information for assessment systems to make decisions concerning the validity of testing of ELL students. This literature has examined, for example, the extent to which accommodations improve the performance of ELL students, reduce the gap between ELL and non-ELL students that is attributable to language proficiency, preserve the constructs tests are intended to measure, are relevant to the characteristics of the recipients, and are easy to implement (Abedi, 2012; Cawthon, Leppo, Carr, & Kopriva, 2013; Sireci, Li, & Scarpati, 2003).

Table 7.2 summarizes the characteristics of accommodations for which there is a reasonable body of research on their effectiveness, as reflected by a reduction in the score gap between ELL and non-ELL students (see also Wolf, Kao, Herman, *et al.*, 2008). These accommodations can be characterized as defensible because they provide linguistic support in the sense that they are intended to address language factors.

Findings on the effectiveness of the accommodations shown in Table 7.2 are inconsistent or difficult to generalize (see Penock-Roman & Rivera, 2011). In part, this is inconsistency is due to the fact that each accommodation is in actuality a category or family of accommodations whose characteristics may vary across investigations (see Abedi, Lord, & Plummer, 1997; Abedi, Courtney & Leon, 2003; Abedi, Lord, Boscardin, & Miyoshi, 2001). For example, there are many ways in which *linguistic simplification* can be understood—from simply editing the text of items to substantially modifying the text based on analyses of lexical frequency and other properties of text.

TABLE 7.2 Characteristics of Some Accommodations for Which There is Empirical Evidence of Effectiveness in ELL Testing. Based on Abedi and Ewers (2013) and Sireci and Faulkner-Bond (2015).

Linguistic Simplification	The text of items is simplified by reducing sentence length, replacing words of low frequency or words that are morphologically complex, editing sentences with unusual syntactical structure or embedded clauses, etc. The intent is to minimize reading load without changing terms that are part of the content being assessed.
Dictionary	Students are provided with a dictionary containing definitions of words. The range of forms of dictionary vary, from a standard, commercially available dictionary, to a dictionary with definitions in simplified English, to a dictionary customized to the test.
Glossary	Students are provided with definitions of certain words. The definitions may be provided in a booklet along with the test, next to each item, or, in computer-administered tests, as definitions that pop up on the screen when the student clicks on certain words.
Translated Glossary	Students are provided with translations of certain words. The translations may be provided in a booklet along with the test, next to each item, or, in computer-administered tests, as translations which pop up on the screen when the student clicks on certain words.
Translated Test	Students are provided with a translation of the test in their native language. The translation may replace the original text in English or may appear next to it in a dual (side-by-side) format.
Extra time	Students are giving additional time to complete their tests with the intent to give them the opportunity to work through the linguistic demands posed by items administered in their second language. Typically, extra time is provided in combination with other forms of accommodations.

Research has found that, while accommodations do not necessary alter the constructs measured by tests, they are only moderately effective or not effective in their ability to reduce the score gap between ELL and non-ELL students (Kieffer, Lesaux, Rivera, & Francis, 2009; Penock-Roman & Rivera, 2011).

English glossaries and dictionaries are the forms of accommodation that tend produce statistically significant increases in the score of ELL students, although their contribution to reducing this score gap is minimal (Kieffer, Lesaux, Rivera, & Francis, 2009).

Variation in the Development and Use of Testing Accommodations

One reason that accounts for the limited effectiveness of testing accommodations for ELL students has to do with the tremendous variation in which accommodations are understood, developed, and used. Practice concerning testing accommodations for ELL students appears to be guided by the implicit assumption that the same given accommodation is interpreted and used in the same way by different educators and test administrators in different contexts. This assumption may mislead to flawed generalizations on the effectiveness of accommodations. A case in point is the linguistic simplification of test items. For example, if different teams of professionals with the same qualifications and training are asked to simplify the linguistic features of the same item, most likely they will produce different versions of the item, even if they use the same linguistic simplification procedure. These differences should caution assessment systems against holding unrealistic expectations about the power of testing accommodations to ensure validity and fair testing for ELL students.

Unfortunately, assessment policies do not provide sufficient information to insure that testing accommodations are implemented consistently. For example, while the National Assessment Governing Board provides guidelines for the inclusion of ELL students in NAEP (the National Assessment of Educational Progress), states' assessment systems vary on the types of and levels of accommodation they provide for their ELLs (National Center for Education Statistics, 2009). Thus, NAEP authorizes the use of Spanish translations of tests for ELL students who are native Spanish users (except for the reading test) but it does not provide guidance about the qualifications of the individuals who are to translate the tests or the translation procedures that should be used. In addition, there are factors that may affect the quality of test translations. For example, individuals in charge of translating tests may not be given the time they need to review and refine their work carefully and to try it out with samples of target students (see Stansfield, 2003). With this lack of consistency of procedures, it is difficult to ensure comparability of measures of academic achievement for ELL students across states or school districts.

Sensitivity to Linguistic Heterogeneity

Another reason that accounts for the limited effectiveness of testing accommodations for ELL students has to do with the heterogeneity of ELL populations. Research and practice concerning testing accommodations for ELL students appears to be guided by the implicit assumption that accommodations work in the same way for all students, as though ELL populations were homogeneous. The validity of that research and testing practices may be threatened by heterogeneity on factors such as first language and different schooling histories when those factors are not properly controlled for (Abedi & Ewers, 2013).

Due to this lack of sensitivity to linguistic heterogeneity, blanket approaches, in which the same set of accommodations is given to all ELL students, may be ineffective (Abedi, Hofstetter, & Lord, 2004). Moreover, because tests of English proficiency may render false positive and false negative classifications of students according to English proficiency (see Chapter 4), blanket testing accommodation policies may have devastating effects for ELL students who have been misclassified. For example, a translated version of a test may be far from benefitting a student who has always been in English-only programs and who has developed reading and writing skills and academic language in English. Unfortunately, in many cases, accurate, updated information on the exact schooling history of the students and many other factors that contribute to linguistic heterogeneity may not be available.

A worrying sign that practice in the field of accommodations has not effectively addressed the complexities of language and linguistic groups is that many reports on the effectiveness of testing accommodations do not include critical information on the characteristics of ELL participants. The absence of this information limits the interpretability of the results and limits the effectiveness of accommodations. For example, there is evidence that, unless they are assigned to students based on detailed information on their proficiency in English in different language modes, accommodations are as effective as if they were assigned randomly to students (Kopriva, Emick, Hipolito-Delgado, & Cameron, 2007).

Questionable Testing Accommodations

An important source of concern in current testing practices stems from the fact that many testing accommodations that are part of institutionalized testing practice lack any empirical support. Thus, of the total of 44 testing accommodations used by states to test ELL students (Rivera, Collum, Willner, Sia, & Ku, 2006), only those shown in Table 7.2 have been sufficiently investigated (see Abedi & Ewers, 2013; Sireci & Faulkner-Bond, 2015).

An aggravating circumstance that threatens validity and fairness in ELL testing is the fact that two-thirds of the states' assessment policies tend to list accommodations for ELL students and accommodations for students with disabilities together (Rivera & Collum, 2004). For some accommodations, it is clear that the target recipients are students with disabilities (e.g. "test interpreted for the deaf or hearing impaired/use of sign language provided"). However, other accommodations intended for students with disabilities are likely to be misinterpreted as being meant for ELL students (e.g. "test-taker dictates or uses a scribe to respond in English," "enlarged print," "test-taker provided preferential seating," "special/appropriate lighting provided"). As stated by Rivera and Collum, by including accommodations for ELL students and accommodations for students with disabilities together, "states' policies ignore important differences between ELLs and students with disabilities and encourage the perception that the needs of all 'special populations' can be met through the same assessment strategies" (Rivera & Collum, 2004, p. 20).

Increasing the Effectiveness of Test Taking Support Devices

Attempts to increase the effectiveness of test taking support devices for ELL students have been guided by two forms of reasoning—deterministic and probabilistic. While researchers' and test developers' practices tend to reflect one or the other, these two forms of reasoning should be thought of as mutually complementary, rather than antithetical.

Deterministic Approaches

Deterministic approaches attempt to address the linguistic heterogeneity of ELL populations by gathering and using as much information as possible about each student's proficiency in English (Abedi & Ewers, 2013; Kopriva & Koran, 2008). Based on a deterministic reasoning, serious efforts have been made to develop computerized decision-making systems intended to identify different patterns of proficiency in English and to match each ELL student with the optimal set of accommodations and accessibility resources.

While the technology needed to develop these decision-making systems exists, their implementation may be costly mainly because they require collecting information on the students' proficiency in English from multiple sources. In addition, these deterministic approaches are silent about the variability in the ways in which accommodations and accessibility resources are developed and implemented. As a result, even if a student is assigned, for example, to the optimal set of accommodations according to accurate information available on their proficiency in English, the quality of the accommodations and the fidelity with which these accommodations are implemented may not be optimal.

Probabilistic Approaches

In contrast, *probabilistic approaches* recognize that the information on English proficiency for each ELL student is imperfect and fragmented. It also recognizes that accommodations may be flawed and poorly implemented. When a probabilistic reasoning on testing accommodations and accessibility resources is used, the focus is on the interaction of the student and the test taking support device.

From a probabilistic standpoint, the effectiveness of a test taking support device depends on both the characteristics of the students and the level of fidelity with which testing accommodations or accessibility resources are likely to be implemented (Solano-Flores, 2014; Solano-Flores & Trumbull, 2008).

Whereas the notion of probability is at the core of the field of educational measurement, policy and practice concerning test taking support devices have not been guided significantly by probabilistic reasoning. Students' skills are assumed to be properly classified and fidelity of implementation is not questioned. Only recently, some testing models have been developed according to which the effectiveness of an accommodation or accessibility resource is evaluated in terms of the magnitude of measurement error that it contributes to reduce (Solano-Flores & Li, 2013). This approach contrasts with the conventional approach in which the effectiveness of an accommodation is evaluated in terms of the differences of scores between students who are and students who are not given the accommodation.

Selecting and Using Test Taking Support Devices

Given the multiple factors that shape the effectiveness of test taking support devices, attempting to identify the accommodations or accessibility resources that are effective under any set of circumstances appears to be a fruitless endeavor. Reasoning about the characteristics of test taking support devices and how they work given the characteristics of specific students and under a given set of circumstances appears to be more productive.

This section offers a set of criteria intended to help educators to think critically about the possibilities and limitations of test taking support devices in relation to their ELL students. The criteria also should be helpful for educators to have realistic expectations about the extent to which these test taking support devices can minimize limited English proficiency as a threat to test validity and fairness. Table 7.3 shows a summary of these criteria, which are stated as questions.

Needless to say, there are important commonalities between the set of criteria discussed in this section and the set of criteria typically used to inform assessment systems with regard to the testing of ELLs (e.g. Abedi, 2012). What makes this set of criteria different is that they allow educators to reason about how effectively a given accommodation may work for their own ELL students or about the optimal combination of accessibility resources for a given specific ELL student.

Some of the criteria were developed as part of a framework created to help test developers to reason about the possibilities and limitations of different forms of translations for ELLs, including full text, translated glossaries, and dual language (side-by-side) versions of a test (Solano-Flores, 2012). This set of criteria has been expanded, so that it can be used by educators to analyze a wide variety of test taking support devices.

TABLE 7.3 Criteria for Evaluating Fairness and Validity of Test Taking Support Devices. Based on Solano-Flores (2012).

Safety of untargeted test takers: Is the test taking support device safe when it is given by mistake to students who do not need it?

Sensitivity to individual test takers' needs: Does the test taking support device react according to the actions of each individual student in support of their specific needs?

Sensitivity to the characteristics of items: Does the test taking support device react in a way that the information it provides is specific to the linguistic features and the context of the items?

Fidelity of implementation: Is the test taking support device likely to be provided to students with ease in the way in which it is intended to be provided, regardless of the qualifications of the persons responsible for providing it or the conditions in which the test is administered?

Usability: Can the test taking support device be used by the test taker with ease, without having to make a substantial effort to understand how to use it?

Safety of Untargeted Test Takers

Certain test taking support devices may be harmful rather than beneficial to students who do not need them. For example, tests administered in the students' native language may be effective in supporting students who have a history of schooling in their first language or who have been in bilingual programs in which the content is taught in their first language. In contrast, they may be harmful for students who have a history of schooling only in English. Even if ELL students are fluent speakers of their first language, they do not necessarily have an academic linguistic repertoire in their first language or their reading skills in their first language are unlikely to be as strong as their reading skills in English. As discussed in Chapter 4, classifications of students according to their level of proficiency are not perfect—they may render false positive and false positive cases. Thus, test taking support devices should always be selected keeping in mind that the information or assumptions about the students' proficiency in English and in their first language may be inaccurate.

Sensitivity to Individual Test Takers' Needs

A test taking support device is effective to the extent to which it is capable of supporting any given ELL student's needs. This sensitivity to the student's needs has two aspects: (1) the extent to which the student has the option to use the test taking support device only when it is needed, and (2) the ability of the test taking support device to react to the student's actions. For example, in paper-and-pencil tests, illustrations can be added to items originally created without an illustration with the intent to support students in making sense of the text of those items (Solano-Flores, Wang, Kachchaf, Soltero-Gonzalez, &

Nguyen-Le, 2014). The assumption underlying this testing accommodation is that the illustrations will be used only by those students who may benefit from an additional form of representation of some aspects of the information provided by the text of the items. However, these illustrations are static; they do not react to the specific actions of the students. In contrast, imagine an accessibility resource consisting of pop-up illustrations in computer-administered testing. On the screen of the computer, in the text of an item, certain terms which are irrelevant to the construct measured are highlighted. For example, a dotted line below a term indicates that an illustration for that term is available. When the student clicks on it, a pop-up window appears with an illustration of the term (Chía, 2015). Clearly, this accessibility resource has the capability to react according to each student's needs.

Sensitivity to the Characteristics of Items

To be effective, test taking support devices need to be sensitive to the specific sets of linguistic challenges posed by items. Think about a commercially available dictionary. Suppose that a student needs to look for the definition of the word *even*. The dictionary may provide several definitions of the word, which has more than one meaning.

Unless the student has the metalinguistic skills needed to evaluate how each definition fits the context of the text containing the word, the dictionary is likely to fail to provide the kind of support needed. In contrast, item-specific glossaries are considerably more sensitive to the specific linguistic challenges posed by a given item. They provide, for each item, a list of terms and their definitions or translations for selected terms identified as likely to pose challenges to ELL students.

Fidelity of Implementation

To be fair and to effectively contribute to valid interpretations of test scores, a test taking support device should be provided or made available as intended. For example, the fidelity of implementation of an accommodation consisting of reading aloud the items of a test in the student's native language may be limited by the availability of professionals who are able to speak that language. Even if those professionals are available, they may vary tremendously on their oral proficiency and their knowledge of the cultural factors that shape that language's usage (e.g. subtle but important dialect differences). In contrast, illustrations added to the text of items, pop-up illustrations, glossaries with translations of specific terms, and pop-up glossaries are likely to be implemented with fidelity because their use is not affected by the circumstances in which students are tested.

The implementation of a test taking support device (especially an accommodation) is effective to the extent to which it is not based on assumptions about the skills of the individuals in charge of providing it.

Usability

The term *usability* refers to the extent to which an individual can use an object or device with ease (Norman, 2013). Based on this notion, to a great extent, the effectiveness of a test taking support device depends on the realism of the assumptions made about the ease with which ELL students will use it. If these assumptions are erroneous, test taking support devices may be not likely to help these students to gain accesses to the content of items.

Suppose that ELL students are provided with a commercially available dictionary—a book with a list of words alphabetically ordered and the definitions of those words. Underlying the use of this accessibility resource is the assumption that the student is able to perform alphabetical searches with ease. While this form of accommodation may work, say, for educated adults who take a test in a second language, it may not work for students living in the US. In an era of Internet, search engines, and electronic dictionaries, academic curricula may not emphasize word searching skills as strongly as these skills were taught and valued in the past.

If the usability of a test taking support device is low, students have to struggle figuring out how to benefit from it and may need to be given directions and time to practice before they can become sufficiently familiar with the device. This may affect their overall performance on a test.

A good way of thinking about the usability of a test taking support device is in terms of the extent to which students can use it intuitively with little or no directions. Pop-up glossaries and pop-up illustrations can be designed in ways that are similar to clicking hyperlinks in the Internet, thus requiring from students to interact with the computer in ways that are familiar to them (e.g. recognizing when a glossary or illustration is available for a given term; clicking on the term to make the glossary or illustration pop up; clicking on the pop-up illustration or glossary to make it disappear).

Another way of thinking about usability is in terms of cognitive load. As discussed in Chapter 3, cognitive load refers to the amount and complexity of information that a person needs to process simultaneously before being able to make sense of a situation or solve a problem. Any test taking support device necessarily imposes a cognitive load inherent to figuring out or recognizing how to use it (e.g. performing an alphabetical search, clicking on a word for which a translation is available) and to processing the information provided by the device (e.g. making sense of a translation or a definition). Needless to say, the best test taking support device is that which provides the maximum information needed for the student to make sense of items without imposing a substantial cognitive load increase.

Closing Comments

Providing support for ELL students to overcome the linguistic challenges of items that are not related to the content being assessed is a simple notion. Yet there is a limit to the power of accommodations and accessibility resources to minimize English proficiency as a factor that threatens validity in the testing of ELL students.

Unfortunately, the inclusion of ELLs in large-scale state and national assessment systems appears to be based on the false premise that all testing accommodations and accessibility resources are highly effective under any circumstances. Educators need to have realistic expectations about the ability of testing accommodations and accessibility resources to effectively support their ELL students. Understanding the limitations and possibilities of test taking support devices enables educators to select the best set of accessibility resources for each of their ELL students.

Exercises

Exercise 7.1: Evaluating Testing Accommodations

1. Find a commercially available dictionary in printed form. List all the features that might make it difficult for ELL students to benefit from an accommodation consisting of simply giving them a commercially available dictionary.
2. If you were to edit the dictionary to make it more likely to support ELL in gaining access to the content of items, what changes would make? Why?
3. Suppose that you and your colleagues decide to create glossaries with brief translations of words that are challenging to ELL students in different grades. How will you determine which words are to be included and which ones are to be excluded? Propose and justify at least three criteria that you would use to select the words systematically.
4. Using the format shown in Figure 7.1, rate each of the three testing support devices as low, medium, and high on each of the five validity and fairness criteria. Write your rating in the corresponding cell and provide the rationale for your rating.
5. Based on your ratings, make a decision on the validity and fairness of the testing support devices. Overall, which of the three forms of accommodations would be better for your ELL students? Why?

	Validity and Fairness Criteria				
Accommodation/ Accessibility Resource	Safety of Untargeted Test Takers	Sensitivity to Individual Test Takers' Needs	Sensitivity to the Characteristics of Items	Fidelity of Implementation	Usability
Commercially available dual-language dictionary with English words translated to first language (paper-and-pencil tests)					
Glossary with definitions in English of the terms used in each item (paper-and pencil tests)					
Pop-up glossary with translations of terms (computer administered tests)					

FIGURE 7.1 Format for evaluating test taking support devices.

Exercise 7.2: Testing Accommodations and Validity

1. Make an attempt to read the sentence that appears below.
   剧烈的气候变化可能在恐龙灭绝的过程中起到了巨大的作用。
2. Assuming that you are not a Chinese native user, most likely you cannot read what the sentence says. Would you be able to understand the sentence under enhanced lighting conditions and if it were provided to you in enlarged print? Explain why.
3. Lighting conditions and enlarged print are among the testing accommodations for students with disabilities that some states' policies list along with testing accommodations for ELLs. This can mislead school districts, schools, or educators, in their decisions concerning the testing support devices that are appropriate for their ELL students. Discuss, in terms of validity and fairness, at least three reasons why including accommodations for ELL students along with accommodations for students with disabilities is not appropriate.

Exercise 7.3: Cognitive Load and Test Taking Support Devices

1. Test taking support devices can potentially help ELL students to gain access to the content of items. At the same time, they impose a cognitive load for the test taker. Discuss the potential cognitive load for each of the following two test taking support devices:
   - Students tested with paper-and-pencil tests are given a bilingual, side-by-side test. On the left side, the items appear in the students' first language; on the right side, the same items appear in English. Test takers are supposed to switch back and forth between language versions to make sense of the items. For example, when they find a word or an expression they do not understand in English, they can look for that word or expression in the first language version of the item.
   - Students tested with computers are given multiple accessibility resources together. When they click on a word or phrase, three boxes are displayed on the screen at the same time. One shows the translation in the students' first language. Another shows a pictorial representation of the word or phrase. The third box shows a definition of the word or phrase in English.

Exercise 7.4: Defensibility of Testing Accommodations

1. Below is a list of some of the accommodations that Rivera and Collum (2006) report some states use with ELL students. The accommodations are referred to by Rivera and Collum as Testing Conditions accommodations:
   - Test administered in small group
   - Teacher faces student
   - Test administered in location with minimal distraction
   - Student-provided preferential seating
   - Student takes test in separate location
   - Test administered in ESL/Bilingual classroom
2. Discuss the defensibility of each accommodation. Make sure your discussion addresses:
   - How the accommodation is supposed to support the student to gain access to the content of items
   - The specific aspects of language proficiency to which the accommodation appears to be sensitive

Note

Note 7.1. As mentioned in the overview of this chapter, the distinction between accommodation and accessibility is not always clear and varies depending on the criteria used to distinguish between these categories. Because of this inconsistency, dictionaries and glossaries have been treated as accommodations in the literature on accommodations but are discussed here as accessibility resources.

References

Abedi, J. (2012). Validity issues in designing accommodations. In G. Fulcher & F. Davidson (Eds.), *The Routledge handbook of language testing in a nutshell*. Florence, KY: Routledge, Taylor & Francis Group.

Abedi, J. (2014). The use of computer technology in designing appropriate test accommodations for English language learners. *Applied Measurement in Education, 27*(4) 261–272.

Abedi, J. & Ewers, N. (2013). *Accommodations for English language learners and students with disabilities: A research-based decision algorithm*. Smarter Balanced Assessment Consortium. Retrieved June 15, 2015 from http://www.smarterbalanced. org/wordpress/wp-content/uploads/2012/08/Accomodations-for-under-represented-students.pdf.

Abedi, J., Courtney, M., & Leon, S. (2003). *Research-supported accommodation for English language learners in NAEP*. (CSE Tech. Rep. No. 586). Los Angeles: University of California, National Center for Research on Evaluation, Standards, and Student Testing.

Abedi, J., Hofstetter, C., & Lord, C. (2004). Assessment accommodations for English language learners: Implications for policy-based empirical research. *Review of Educational Research, 74*(1), 1–28.

Abedi, J., Lord, C., & Plummer, J. R. (1997). *Final report of language background as a variable in NAEP mathematics performance*. CSE Technical Report 429. Los Angeles: UCLA Center for the Study of Evaluation/National Center for Research on Evaluation, Standards, and Student Testing.

Abedi, J., Lord, C., Boscardin, C. K., & Miyoshi, J. (2001). *The effects of accommodations on the assessment of LEP students in NAEP*. Los Angeles: University of California, National Center for Research on Evaluation, Standards, and Student Testing.

Abedi, J., Lord, C., Hofstetter, C., & Baker, E. (2001). Impact of accommodation strategies on English language learners' test performance. *Educational Measurement: Issues and Practice, 19*(3), 16–26.

Cawthon, S., Leppo, R., Carr, T., & Kopriva, R. (2013). Toward accessible assessments: The promises and limitations of test item adaptations for students with disabilities and English language learners. *Educational Assessment, 18*, 73–98.

Chía, M. (2015). *Smarter Balanced: an online assessment measuring the new CCSS while meeting students' individual needs*. Symposium paper presented at the annual conference of the American Educational Research Association. Chicago, IL, April.

Kieffer, M. J., Lesaux, N. K., Rivera, M., & Francis, D. J. (2009). Accommodations for English language learners taking large-scale assessments: A meta-analysis on effectiveness and validity. *Review of Educational Research, 79*(3), 1168–1201.

Kopriva, R. J., Emick, J. E., Hipolito-Delgado, C. P., & Cameron, C. A. (2007). Do proper accommodation assignments make a difference? Examining the impact of improved decision making on scores for English language learners. *Educational Measurement: Issues and Practice, 26*(3), 11–20.

Kopriva, R. & Koran, J. (2008). Proper assignment of accommodations to individual students. In R. J. Kopriva (Ed.), *Improving testing for English language learners: A comprehensive approach to designing, building, implementing and interpreting better academic assessments* (pp. 217–254). New York: Routledge.

Measured Progress & ETS Collaborative (2012). *Smarter Balanced Assessment Consortium: General accessibility guidelines*. April 16, 2012. Retrieved June 15, 2015 from http://www.smarterbalanced.org/wordpress/wp-ontent/uploads/2012/05/ TaskItemSpecifications/Guidelines/AccessibilityandAccommodations/ GeneralAccessibilityGuidelines.pdf

Measured Progress & National Center on Educational Outcomes (2014). *Smarter Balanced Assessment Consortium: Accessibility and accommodations framework*. http:// www.google.com/url?sa=t&rct=j&q=&esrc=s&source=web&cd=2&ved= 0CCMQFjAB&url=http%3A%2F%2Fwww.smarterbalanced.org%2 Fwordpress%2Fwpcontent%2Fuploads%2F2014%2F02%2FAccessibility-and- Accommodations-Framework.pdf&ei=MBXuU7f4ENKAygT05IKgBA& usg=AFQjCNGGXEiowp4tIzGTMLy1mIJQfmrgEw&bvm=bv.73231344, d.aWw

National Center for Education Statistics (2009). *The Nation's Report Card: An Overview of Procedures for the NAEP Assessment* (NCES 2009–493) US Department of Education. Institute of Education Sciences. National Center for Education Statistics. Washington, DC: US Government Printing Office.

Norman, D. (2013). *The design of everyday things: Revised and expanded edition.* New York: Basic Books.

Penock-Roman, M. & Rivera, C. (2011). Mean effects of test accommodations for ELLs and non-ELLs: A meta-analysis of experimental studies. *Educational Measurement: Issues and Practice, 30*(3), 10–28.

Rivera, C. & Collum, E. (Eds.) (2006). *State assessment policy and practice for English language learners: A national perspective*. Mahwah, NJ: Lawrence Earlbaum Associates.

Rivera, C. & Collum, E. (2004). An analysis of state assessment policies addressing the accommodation of English language learners: Commissioned Paper Synopsis. *NAGB Conference on Increasing the Participation of SD and LEP Students in NAEP.* The George Washington University, Center for Equity and Excellence in Education.

Rivera, C., Collum, E., Willner, L. N., & Sia, Jr., J. K. (2006). Study 1: An analysis of state assessment policies regarding the accommodation of English language learners. In C. Rivera & E. Collum (Eds.), *State assessment policy and practice for English language learners: A national perspective* (pp. 1–136). Mahwah, NJ: Lawrence Erlbaum Associates, Publishers.

Sireci, S. G. & Faulkner-Bond, M. (2015). Promoting validity in the assessment of English learners. *Review of Research in Education, 39*, 215–252.

Sireci, S. G., Li, S., & Scarpati, S. (2003). *The effects of test accommodation on test performance: A review of the literature* (Research Report 485). Amherst, MA: Center for Educational Assessment.

Smarter Balanced Assessment Consortium (2014). Usability, accessibility, and accommodations guidelines. Prepared with the assistance of the National Center on Educational Outcomes. March 9, 2015. Retrieved April 15, 2015 from http://www.smarterbalanced.org/wordpress/wp-content/uploads/2014/08/SmarterBalanced_Guidelines.pdf.

Solano-Flores, G. (2014). Probabilistic approaches to examining linguistic features of test items and their effect on the performance of English language learners. *Applied Measurement in Education. 27*(4), 236–247.

Solano-Flores, G. (2012). *Translation accommodations framework for testing English language learners in mathematics.* Developed for the Smarter Balanced Assessment Consortium (SBAC). September 18, 2012. Retrieved June 15, 2015 from http://www.smarterbalanced.org/wordpress/wp-content/uploads/2012/09/Translation-Accommodations-Framework-for-Testing-ELL-Math.pdf.

Solano-Flores, G. & Li, M. (2013). Generalizability theory and the fair and valid assessment of linguistic minorities. *Educational Research and Evaluation, 19*(2–3), 245–263.

Solano-Flores, G. & Trumbull, E. (2008). In what language should English language learners be tested? In R. J. Kopriva (Ed.), *Improving testing for English language learners: A comprehensive approach to designing, building, implementing and interpreting better academic assessments* (pp. 169–200). New York: Routledge.

Solano-Flores, G., Shade, C., & Chrzanowski, A. (2014). *Item accessibility and language variation conceptual framework.* Submitted to the Smarter Balanced Assessment Consortium. October 10. Retrieved July 30, 2015 from http://www.smarterbalanced.org/wordpress/wp-content/uploads/2014/11/ItemAccessibilityandLanguageVariationConceptualFramework_11-10.pdf.

Solano-Flores, G., Wang, C., Kachchaf, R., Soltero-Gonzalez, L., & Nguyen-Le, K. (2014). Developing testing accommodations for English language learners: Illustrations as visual supports for item accessibility. *Educational Assessment, 19*, 267–283.

Stansfield, C. W. (2003). Test translation and adaptation in public education in the USA. *Language Testing, 20*, 188–206.

Wolf, M. K., Kao, J. C., Herman, J., Bachman, L. F., Bailey, A. L., Bachman, P. L., Farnsworth, T., & Chang, S. M. (2008). *Issues in assessing English language learners: English language proficiency measures and accommodation uses: Literature review (Part 1 of 3).* CRESST Report 731. National Center for Research on Evaluation, Standards, and Student Testing, Graduate School of Education & Information, University of California, Los Angeles.

8

CONTENT AND RESPONSE PROCESSES

Overview

This chapter discusses test review—the examination of the characteristics of items with the intent to ensure to meet standards of technical quality—with regard to the assessment of ELL students. Test review is discussed as an activity that promotes critical thinking about test instruments and helps educators to address the complex interaction between the characteristics of test items and the characteristics of students.

The section "The Importance of Test Review" discusses the main goals of test review and presents a simple classification of types of test review. It also discusses the importance for teachers to use review procedures to examine the characteristics of test items as critical to valid and fair assessment for ELL students.

The section "Test Review Focused on Content" discusses how judgments about the quality of test items can be made based on their complexity and the ways in which they appear to be aligned to the content of normative standards or consistent with the ways in which content is taught in the classroom.

The section "Test Review Focused on Response Processes" discusses test item quality based on the cognitive processes underlying the ways in which students make sense of test items and respond to them. These cognitive processes are inferred from empirical information on students' verbalizations or descriptions of their thinking while they engage in solving problems. Also, they are based on examining the students' actions or responses to items.

The Importance of Test Review

Defining Test Review

Test review can be defined as the set of activities oriented to examining the characteristics of tests and items and identifying ways in which tests need to be improved to ensure that they meet certain standards of technical quality. Test review pays attention to multiple aspects of items, such as content, difficulty, and fairness (see Hambleton & Jirka, 2006; Zieky, 2006). It may reveal the need for revising the wording or layout of some items or even the need for discarding some items from a test's item pool.

Ultimately, test review concerns validity, as it involves consideration of multiple forms of validity evidence and the extent to which multiple pieces of evidence and theory support a given interpretation of scores for specific uses (AERA, APA, NCME, 2014). Test review is intimately related to *validation*, the term used to refer to the evaluation of the rationale, arguments, and evidence in support of claims that a test measures a given construct (Kane, 2006).

Needless to say, while test review is always important in the assessment of any population of students, it is especially important in the assessment of ELL students. Yet, unfortunately, assessments are commonly developed with mainstream populations in mind. Rarely during the process of development of tests are ELL students included as pilot participants with whom ongoing versions of the items are tried out, for example to detect unnecessary linguistic complexity. Typically, test review, as it relates to issues related to ELL students, takes place towards the end of the process of assessment development. As a consequence, the stage of test review may be the only opportunity to ensure fairness and validity in the assessment of ELL students, for example, by taking actions that are likely to minimize bias against ELL students due to culture or language issues.

Procedures for reviewing tests are classified into two categories, empirical and judgmental (see Gierl, Rogers, & Klinger, 1999; Hambleton & Jones, 1994; Solano-Flores & Kidron, 2006). Unlike those classifications, for the purposes of this book, three types of test review are identified: test review focused on evidence on content, test review procedures focused on evidence on response processes, and test review focused on the relations of the scores of a test scores with other variables (Figure 8.1). The classification is consistent with three forms of evidence considered in examining the validity of interpretations of information produced by tests (AERA, APA, & NCME, 2014). Test review focused on evidence on content and test review focused on evidence on response processes are discussed in this section. Test review focused on the relations of test scores with other variables are discussed in Chapter 9, along with other properties of tests.

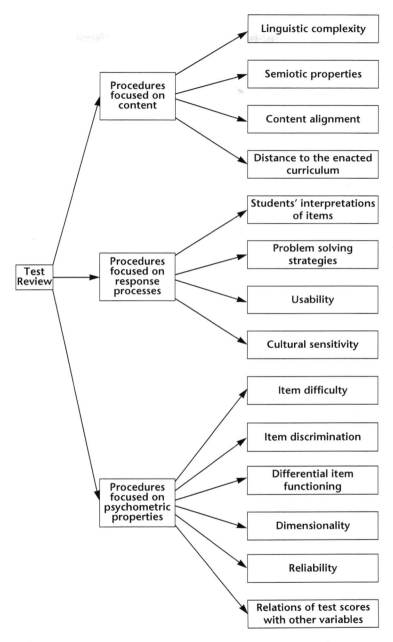

FIGURE 8.1 Types of test review procedures particularly relevant in the assessment of ELL students and the information they produce.

Teachers as Test Reviewers

Test review reveals the complex interaction between the characteristics of items and the students' reasoning. Educators can capitalize on experience and procedures from the field of test review to develop strategies for judging the characteristics of test items in ways that best serve their assessment needs and the needs of their ELL students.

Being familiar with test review procedures helps educators to be critical users of tests at least in two ways. First, it equips them with the knowledge needed to properly examine the complexity of test items, the multiple ways in which test items may be flawed, and the limitations of tests that need to be considered in using test scores to make decisions about students.

Being familiar with test review procedures also helps educators to develop the habit of reasoning about the cognitive processes underlying students' responses to test items. For example, educators become aware of the ways in which the linguistic features of test items and the contextual information provided by these items influence the students' interpretations of items.

Test Review Focused on Content

The term *content* refers to the multiple aspects of tests items, such as wording, themes, and format, and the guidelines for administration and scoring of a test (AERA, APA, & NCME, 2014). Thus, *test review focused on content* is based on information on both the textual and non-textual characteristics of items and the extent to which those characteristics may affect the validity of interpretations of test scores. Test review focused on content is important because high costs and tight timelines may pose a limit to the amount of time and resources that test developers can use to gather empirical evidence of the properties of all items with multiple segments of the population of examinees (e.g. male and female students; mainstream, native English speaking and ELL students).

In research and in large-scale assessment contexts, review procedures focused on content are performed by panels of professionals with different kinds of expertise. Typically, test review panels are conformed by content experts (e.g. scientists for a science assessment), curriculum experts, and teachers. These professionals discuss and evaluate the items according to guidelines that address aspects such as the extent to which the items match the item specifications, the soundness of their design, and their clarity, accessibility, readability, and fairness (Welch, 2006). Ideally, review panels should include also linguists, bilingual educators, and teachers with ample experience teaching ELL students.

Four item properties are especially important in the assessment of ELL students: linguistic complexity, semiotic properties, content alignment, and distance to the enacted curriculum.

Linguistic Complexity

Not a surprise, linguistic complexity is critical to minimizing limited proficiency in English as a threat to valid testing for ELL students. However, as mentioned in Chapter 7, while there is evidence that simplifying the linguistic features of test items contributes to reducing the score gap between ELL and non-ELL students, the evidence on the effectiveness of this approach is not impressive (see Kieffer, Lesaux, Rivera, & Francis, 2009).

One possible reason that accounts for this limited effectiveness is that language can be complex in many ways. As an example, consider the item shown below (California Department of Education, 2014):

> An athlete can run 9 kilometers in 1 hour. If the athlete runs at that same average speed for 30 minutes, how far will the athlete travel?

The second sentence of this item is complex; it is a question with a conditional clause. The item could be simplified as follows:

> An athlete can run 9 kilometers in 1 hour. Suppose that the athlete runs at that same average speed for 30 minutes. How far will the athlete travel?

The potential linguistic challenges of the original item are addressed by breaking the second sentence into two sentences. Yet the change has a cost: the amount of text has increased slightly. More importantly, some would argue that questions with conditional clauses are very frequent in science and mathematics textbooks and classrooms (Morgan, 1998). While the second and third sentences in the simplified version are likely to be read with ease, they do not reflect the style of asking questions to which students may be used. Formally, the second version of the item may be simpler; functionally, the simplification may not be as effective as it could be expected.

Guidelines for item writing may attempt to address the challenges of validly testing ELL students by including recommendations such as *avoid the use of double negation* or *avoid excessive verbiage* (see the review by Haladyna, Downing, & Rodriguez, 2002). It is important to keep in mind that, while necessary, these recommendations may not be sufficient to properly address linguistic complexity. Their effectiveness is shaped by the context established by each item and the characteristics of ELL students and their language backgrounds. In performing test reviews, it should not be assumed that valid testing for ELL students can be accomplished by following a simple set of rules concerning wording and style.

Researchers and test developers interested in minimizing the linguistic challenges of tests that are not related to the content assessed have used measures of linguistic complexity, such as the number of words or the number of sentences in an item, and the grammatical complexity of those sentences (Abedi, 2006; Shaftel, Belton-Kocher, Glasnapp, & Poggio, 2006). Nobody can contest the notion that, linguistically, test items should not be unnecessarily complex. In fact, there is evidence that these measures of linguistic complexity are related to the difficulty of items (Abedi, 2006; Abedi, Leon, & Mirocha, 2003). Yet reducing the number of words or sentences is not a guarantee that unnecessary linguistic challenges will be eliminated. Editing a sentence with the intent to reduce the number of words in it may have the undesirable effect of increasing its reading demands and cognitive load due to an increased level of encryption.

Semiotic Properties

Multiple ways of conveying meaning through text and image (Lemke, 2003) shape how individuals make sense of experience. Because, traditionally, semiotics is defined as the study of signs and symbols, the term makes people think about images and anything that is not text as the object of study of the discipline. Yet according to current thinking in the field, the distinction between textual and non-textual information is rather arbitrary (Kress van Leeuwen, 2001). In actuality, the arrangement of "non-textual" information (and the way in which an individual interprets that information) is governed by sets of conventions of visual representation of information (e.g. the arrangement of images from top to bottom and from left to right). A reader does not make meaning of text solely from reading the text, regardless of its appearance. The reader also makes meaning based on the visual arrangement of text. For example, a paragraph indentation, an increase in margin width, and boldface are conventions intended to represent, respectively, that a new idea is being discussed, that something said or written by someone who is not the author is being quoted, or that special attention should be paid to a given term or concept. Strictly speaking, the linguistic properties of items are part of their semiotic properties. However, they are discussed in different sections in this chapter because most of the research on test review has focused on the text of items.

With a few exceptions (Kachchaf, 2011; Martiniello, 2009; Solano-Flores, Wang, Kachchaf, Soltero-Gonzalez, & Nguyen-Le, 2014), scant research has been conducted on the formal properties of items from a semiotic perspective in the context of ELL testing. Some authors recommend the use of pictures as visual resources intended to support ELL students in gaining access to the content of items (see Kopriva, 2008). An important limitation underlying this kind of recommendation is the implicit assumption that pictures are understood by everybody in the same way. In actuality, there is evidence that individuals from some cultures vary in the degree to which they pay attention to objects and backgrounds in pictures (Nisbett & Miyamoto, 2005). Also, there is evidence that assessment systems from different countries may differ on the frequency with which different semiotic resources are used in their items (Wang, 2012).

Moreover, evidence from international test comparisons indicates that depending on the countries' levels of achievement (as reflected by their relative rankings) illustrations appear to support or hamper students' making sense of items (Solano-Flores & Wang, 2015). Furthermore, there is evidence that, while the inclusion of illustrations may support text comprehension, it also may increase the cognitive load of text (Mayer, 2005; Schnotz, 2005).

Altogether, this evidence indicates that all the multiple textual and non-textual forms of representation of information act in combination to influence how students make sense of items. Illustrations have a great potential as a resource for supporting ELL students to gain access to the content of items in both large-scale and classroom assessment. However, items should not be assumed to be more explicit simply because they contain illustrations.

Content Alignment

The term *content alignment* refers to the extent to which the items of a test assess the content they are intended to assess and have the characteristics they are supposed to have (Hermann & Baker, 2005; Koretz, 2008; Porter, 2002; Porter, Smithson, Blank, & Zeidner, 2007; Webb, 2007; Webb, Alt, Ely, & Vesperman, 2005). In the context of large-scale assessment, content alignment studies are conducted to determine the correspondence between the content of an assessment and the content specified by assessment frameworks and sets of standards (e.g. Murphy, Bailey, & Butler, 2006; Sato, Lagunoff, Worth, Bailey, & Butler, 2005) or even the content correspondence between different assessments (e.g. National Assessment Governing Board, 2010).

Typically, alignment studies involve teams of reviewers who examine the items of the test or a sample of those items and make judgments about the alignment of the items with a normative document. The information they provide contributes to answering questions such as the following: *Are the knowledge and skills the test appears to assess specified in the content standards? Are the cognitive demands of the test commensurate to the cognitive demands reflected by the standards?*

While, in the context of large-scale assessment, alignment studies involve the analysis of dozens and even hundreds of items, equivalent questions can be asked in the classroom context for specific sets of items (e.g. state assessment programs' public item releases). These questions make the connection between knowledge and language explicit and help educators to reflect on the linguistic features of items used in large-scale tests. Below are some examples:

- What is the knowledge this item is intended to assess?
- What are the linguistic skills needed to learn this knowledge?
- How does the item elicit the response processes stated by the standards?
- How are the item's cognitive and linguistic demands relevant to the content described by the standards?

- What unnecessary linguistic challenges is the item likely to pose to students?
- How could the item's linguistic features and design be improved?

Answering these questions helps educators to examine critically the characteristics of test items and devise strategies to support their ELL students.

Distance to the Enacted Curriculum

To be meaningful, the information on student achievement produced by tests should be interpreted according to their *distance to the enacted curriculum*—the curriculum taught in class (Schmidt, McKnight, & Raizen, 1996). Classroom assessment activities, state assessments, and national assessments are at different distances to the enacted in the classroom. In terms of the goals assessed, the content taught, and the nature of the tasks given to students, classroom assessment activities and instruments are closer than state assessments to the enacted curriculum; in turn, state assessments are closer than national assessments to the enacted curriculum (Ruiz-Primo, Shavelson, Hamilton, & Klein, 2002). For example, while classroom assessment activities are intended to address instructional, unit, and curriculum goals, large-scale assessments are intended to address national and state standards. Also, unlike large-scale assessments, classroom assessment activities and instruments focus on procedures, topics, and concepts that are similar to the procedures, topics, and concepts taught in class.

The concept of distance to the enacted curriculum allows proper use and interpretation of test scores. For example, students perform better on tests for content that they have been taught by their teachers (Porter, 2002). Assessment activities and instruments that are close to the enacted curriculum are more sensitive than remote, national, or state large-scale assessments to differences in student performance due to instruction (Ruiz-Primo, Shavelson, Hamilton, & Klein, 2002). Accordingly, it is possible to think about assessments that produce information on the content students have had the opportunity to learn and the quality of instruction they have received (Ruiz-Primo, Li, Wills, Giamellaro, Lan, Mason, & Sands, 2012).

While the concept of distance to the enacted curriculum was not created with culturally and linguistically diverse students in mind, it is not difficult to understand that language is a major player in the distance of assessments to the enacted curriculum. Indeed, there is evidence that suggests that a great deal of the students' performance on tests can be accounted for by differences between the language used in class, the language used in textbooks, and the language used in tests (Solano-Flores, 2006). For example, we know that the performance of ELLs tested in English is shaped by whether or not the standard form of English used in tests reflects the kind of language used in the students' communities and classrooms. Using "standard English" in tests does not necessarily ensure fair or valid testing for ELLs or native users of non-standard English dialects.

Test Review Focused on Response Processes

Response processes is the term used to refer to the thought, problem solving strategies, and behavior in which test takers engage when they read, interpret, and respond to test items (AERA, APA, & NCME, 1999; Ercikan, 2006; Pellegrino, Chudowsky, & Glaser, 2001). Response processes are inferred, based on information collected, among many other sources, through interviews and think- and read-aloud protocols, and from examining students' responses to items (Leighton & Gierl, 2007).

The term *test review focused on response processes* is used to refer to the activities intended to examine or infer the students' cognitive activity that take place during testing and which may influence how students make sense of items, what reasoning and strategies they use to solve problems, and how they respond to test items.

Unfortunately, while there is a considerable body of research on response processes, only a small fraction of this research has paid attention to ELLs and culturally diverse groups. The scant literature available on the topic speaks to the value of examining validity beyond the comparability of scores (Young, 2009), especially as it relates to the interpretation of items, problem solving strategies, and usability in the design of test items.

Students' Interpretations of Items

Research on students' interpretations of items has examined the degree of correspondence between the knowledge and reasoning used by students when they respond to test items and the knowledge and reasoning those items are intended to measure (e.g. Baxter, Elder, & Glaser, 1996; Megone, Cai, Silver, & Wang, 1994; Ruiz-Primo, Shavelson, Li, & Schultz, 2001). Cognitive activity can be inferred, for example, from talk-aloud protocols in which students verbaliz their thinking while or after they respond to test items (Ericsson & Simon, 1993). Surprisingly, with important exceptions (e.g. Kachchaf, 2011; Martiniello, 2008; Noble, Rosebery, Suarez, & Warren, 2014; Winter, Kopriva, Chen, & Emick, 2006), cognitive interviews have not been used extensively in research on ELL assessment.

Examining item content from a perspective that takes into account the influence of culture on cognition (Vygostky, 1978) allows identification of the extent to which students make connections between their personal experiences and the content of the items. Analyses of cognitive interviews with students from different cultural groups have revealed that students do not necessarily relate the content of items to knowledge acquired in class (Solano-Flores & Nelson-Barber, 2001). Rather, they may draw on personal experiences from other aspects of their lives (e.g. at home, with friends, having fun) to make sense of items, especially when those items provide contextual information (e.g. characters, stories, and situations intended to make the item meaningful). Students from different cultural groups tend to draw on different sets of experiences when they make sense of items (Solano-Flores & Li, 2009).

There is evidence that the linguistic challenges speakers of non-standard forms of English face when they respond to test items and the potential challenges identified by those students' teachers for the same items are not necessarily the same (Solano-Flores & Gustafson, 2013). Teachers from ethnic minority groups and who taught students from the same ethnic groups were asked to examine test items and identify in them features which could pose unnecessary challenges to their students due to linguistic factors or cultural differences. Also, those teachers' students were asked to read aloud the same items. The analysis of the students' read-alouds revealed that students' interpretations of the items could be misled by a combination of linguistic features (i.e. grammatical, pragmatic) acting in combination. While these students' teachers were well aware of the ways in which linguistic features may mislead students' interpretations of test items, in many cases the linguistic features they identified as potentially problematic were not problematic. In other cases, features which they did not perceive as problematic actually were problematic.

This inconsistency indicates that different sources of information used in test review are sensitive to different ways in which culture and the linguistic features of items influence students' interpretations of items. Different sources of information should be used in combination to make decisions about the aspects in which items can be improved.

Problem Solving Strategies

Research on the ways in which students interpret test items has been mainly based on interviewing students about their reasoning after they respond to test items, or on examining their verbalizations while they engage in solving problems or after they complete the tasks. One of the few investigations comparing linguistic groups as to their problem solving strategies examined how students made sense of items with and without illustrations added to the text of those items with the intent to make the content of those items more accessible. An examination of the students' verbal protocols indicated that non-ELL students used a wider variety of problem solving strategies than ELL students; also, ELL students' cognitive activities were more focused than non-ELL students' cognitive activities on making sense of the items (Kachchaf, 2011).

Consistent with those findings, another investigation on illustrations added to texts with the intent to support students to gain access to the content of items examined whether students interpreted the illustrations in the ways intended by the illustration developers. ELL and non-ELL students were given illustrations with and without the text of the items they were created to accompany and were asked to write what they saw in the illustrations. The results indicate that both ELL and non-ELL students used the illustrations to make sense of the content of the items, but they also used the text of the items to make sense of the illustrations (Solano-Flores, Wang, Kachchaf, Soltero-Gonzalez, & Nguyen-Le, 2014).

Another study that examined ELL students' written responses to the same sets of mathematics items administered in English and in their native language found that students' responses were not consistently high or low when tested in one language or in the other language (Solano-Flores, Lara, Sexton, & Navarrete, 2001). The students' responses varied considerably across items and across languages. In addition, some students used different problem solving strategies on the same items depending on the language in which the test was administered. Consistent with previous research on the students' use of two languages to construct knowledge, the findings suggest that, at least for some ELL students, each language may lend itself better than the other to use different forms of reasoning.

As the three examples show, verbal reports, written reports, and the students' written responses to items are rich sources of information on the ways in which students solve problems. These forms of review should be used regularly in large-scale assessment programs to identify sources of invalidity in the testing of ELL students. At least informally, teachers can use these approaches to investigate how their students think and reason when they solve problems.

Item Usability

An aspect of testing not sufficiently investigated in testing concerns *usability* (discussed also in Chapter 7)—a term originated in the field of cognitive science which refers to the ease with which an object can be used according to its intended function (see Norman, 2013). In a testing situation, the "object" is an item—its textual and non-textual components and their layout. Based on these features, altogether, users—test takers—know what the item is about and how they have to do to provide their responses. A high level of usability minimizes the cognitive load of an item due to factors not related to the content being assessed because students do not to make much effort figuring out what the item asks them to do.

Figure 8.2 shows two forms of the same item intended to assess students' knowledge of the concept of percentage and its representation as a part of a whole. While the two forms contain the same basic information and are intended to assess the same content, Form A may take a little more effort and time than Form B for the students to process the information that is not relevant to the skill assessed. Given the construct assessed, the level of usability seems to be higher for Form B than Form A. The mapping (correspondence) between the numerical information to be processed and the space where the percentages are to be reported is more explicit in Form B than in Form A.

Item usability is important in the testing of ELL students because it is a factor that contributes to minimizing the amount of text needed to provide directions. If their design is optimal, objects one sees for the first time should not need

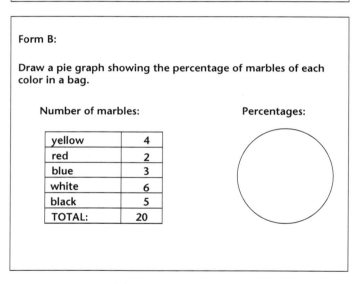

Form A:

A bag contains 20 marbles of the colors shown below:

yellow	red	blue	white	black
4	2	3	6	5

Draw a pie graph showing the percentage of marbles of each color:

Form B:

Draw a pie graph showing the percentage of marbles of each color in a bag.

Number of marbles: Percentages:

yellow	4
red	2
blue	3
white	6
black	5
TOTAL:	20

FIGURE 8.2 Two variations of the same item.

to be accompanied by a set of directions explaining know how to use them (Saffer, 2014). Likewise, well-designed items should not need to provide too many directions for students to be able to understand what they have to do. In a time in which large-scale assessment programs are increasingly administering tests with computers, usability is especially critical to fair and valid testing for ELLs, especially those who live in poverty. Limited access to computers at home may limit students' ability to navigate in the computer interface and to perform actions such as dragging or clicking on objects or interpreting and selecting options from cascade menus.

In the context of large-scale assessment, the extent to which this limited experience with computers may be a threat to validity needs to be determined through studies in which students' interactions with the computer are analyzed. In those studies, students are interviewed about the ways in which they interpret the different components on the computer screen and the challenges they experience understanding what they had to do to respond to the items. Assessment systems should perform routine usability studies with the purpose of improving the design of the different types of items included in their tests.

Usability should not be assumed to be an attribute independent of the characteristics of their users. Personal experience and cultural and linguistic background shape the level of usability of objects. Thus, usability studies should always include representative samples of ELL students.

The experience concerning usability in the context of large-scale assessment can be used to devise ways of investigating the usability of items in the classroom context. As with any form of review focused on response processes, having conversations with ELL students about the characteristics of items that support or hamper their access to the content of items helps educators to develop a sense of the ways in which student performance on tests is shaped by the interaction of the characteristics of the items and the characteristics of the students.

Cultural Sensitivity

Expressions such as being *culturally sensitive*, or *ensuring cultural relevance* or *cultural validity* reflect the recognition that, to be effective, teaching and assessment need to be inclusive and fair and take into account the cultural experiences of students as critical to effective teaching and valid assessment (Gay, 2010; Ladson-Billings, 1995; Solano-Flores, 2011). Practically every assessment system has a procedure in place to perform cultural sensitivity reviews whose main goal is to detect potential sources of bias. Unfortunately, in the context of large-scale assessment, sensitivity review is often times performed towards the end of the entire process of test development—when limited opportunities for substantial transformation of the items are left.

Ultimately, the goal of cultural sensitivity reviews is to ensure that cultural differences between individuals in the population of examinees are properly considered in the design of test items with the intent to ensure fair and valid testing for all students (see Hood, 1998). More specifically, the goal of cultural sensitivity reviews is to detect potential sources of bias in tests. Popham (2012) explains that a test is biased "whenever one or more items on a test offend or unfairly penalize students because of those students' personal characteristics such as race, gender, socioeconomic status, or religion" (p. 6). According to this definition, there are two ways in which an item may be biased. One is when an item, as least in the view of the student, denigrates the group to which the student belongs. The other is when the performance of the students belonging to that group perform is lower than the performance of other students due to aspects of the item that are irrelevant to the construct being assessed.

The characteristics of the procedures for cultural sensitivity review may vary considerably across assessment systems and test developers. Yet all of them are based on having professionals examine test items and make judgments about the items by responding to questions such as *Does the item give a positive representation of* (a given) *cultural group?* and *Is the contextual information provided by the item equally familiar to every cultural group?* (see Hambleton & Rodgers, 1995). In many cases the team of reviewers includes professionals who are members of diverse cultural or ethnic groups.

An important consideration regarding cultural sensitivity is that what reviewers perceive as potentially problematic in items may not actually be a problem when students respond to those items. Or reviewers may fail to identify aspects of items that are indeed problematic. Combining judgmental with empirical approaches may render more precise information concerning cultural sensitivity (Solano-Flores & Trumbull, 2003). In the classroom, teachers can have conversations with their ELL students about the characteristics of the items that may make them feel uncomfortable or which are unfamiliar to them.

Closing Comments

Along with information on the psychometric properties of tests (see Chapter 9), test review renders valuable information on the quality of tests needed to make judgments concerning fair and valid testing for ELL students. The inconsistency of information on the quality of items obtained with procedures focused on content and on response processes is an indication that each form of test review is sensitive to different aspects of the interaction of student and test factors.

Different forms of test review should be used in combination to judge the quality of tests. Based on the experience from research and practice in the field of test review in the context of large-scale assessment, educators can perform their own reviews to develop both a better understanding of their ELL students and how they make sense of items. Also, educators can develop a critical perspective of the complexity of the process involved in test development and test taking.

Exercises

Exercise 8.1: Wording and Problem Structure

1. Below are some problems based on the classic article by De Corte, Verschaffel, & De Win (1985), which reports on an investigation on the wording of mathematics items.

> *David won 13 marbles. Now he has 18 marbles. How many marbles did he have in the beginning?*
>
> *Tom and Annie have 9 candies altogether. Tom has 6 candies. How many candies does Annie have?*
>
> *Jamie has 8 colored pencils. Tori has 3 colored pencils. How many more colored pencils does Jamie have than Tori?*

- How are the problems different or similar?
- Can the three problems be assumed to be exchangeable in terms of the constructs they measure? Why?

2. Select from a public item release one multiple-choice item for the grade you teach and which you think is unnecessarily linguistically complex. Simplify the wording of the item with the intent to make it more accessible to your ELL students.
    - Justify the changes you make. Explain why each specific change makes the item more accessible to your ELL students.
    - Discuss how you would examine whether the changes you made with the intent to reduce the item's linguistic complexity have not created another set of linguistic challenges or increased the item's cognitive load.
    - Discuss how you can examine whether the changes you made with the intent to reduce the item's linguistic complexity have not altered the construct measured.

Exercise 8.2: Distance to the Enacted Curriculum

1. Find in a public release items that correspond to the grade and content you teach.
2. Examine the items in detail and reflect on the extent to which:
    - the items reflect the same topics, concepts and procedures taught in the curriculum;
    - the items are similar to the activities you carry out as part of your teaching of the corresponding topics;
    - the language used in the items (e.g. wording, academic language, expressions, forms of asking questions) reflects the language you use in your teaching; and
    - the forms of representation of information other than text (e.g. figures, charts, formulas, notation) used in the items is similar to or different from the forms of representation information you used in your teaching.

3. Discuss how any differences between the characteristics of the item and the characteristics of enacted curriculum may affect the performance of your students on those tests.
4. Are the differences you found an indication that your teaching should mimic the characteristics of the items and the language used in those tests or an indication that you teaching should promote a wide variety of forms or types of problems and forms of communication? Provide arguments in favor and against.

Exercise 8.3: Usability and Item Design

1. Select from a public item release one constructed-response item for the grade you teach. Make sure that the item contains contextual information and some form of stimulus material (e.g. a passage, a table with data) that the student needs to examine in order to be able to provide a response.
2. Discuss the characteristics of the item in terms of its usability. More specifically, how does the layout of the item and the format provided for students to provide their response minimize or increase the cognitive load that results from attempting to understand what the item is about and how the response has to be provided?
3. Propose an alternative version that increases the usability of the item and justify each change you make.

References

Abedi, J. (2006). Language issues in item development. In S. M. Downing & T. M. Haladyna (Eds.), *Handbook of test development* (pp. 377–398). Mahwah, NJ: Lawrence Erlbaum Associates, Publishers.

Abedi, J., Leon, S., & Mirocha, J. (2003). *Impact of students' language background on content-based assessment: Analyses of extant data* (CSE Tech. Rep. No. 603). Los Angeles: University of California, National Center for Research on Evaluation, Standards, and Student Testing.

American Educational Research Association, American Psychological Association, and National Council for Measurement in Education(1999). *Standards for Educational and Psychological Testing.* Washington, DC: Author.

American Educational Research Association, American Psychological Association, and National Council for Measurement in Education(2014). *Standards for Educational and Psychological Testing.* Washington, DC: Author.

Baxter, G. P., Elder, A. D., & Glaser, R. (1996). Knowledge-based cognition and performance assessment in the science classroom. *Educational Psychologist, 31*(2), 133–140.

California Department of Education (2014). California Standards Tests released test questions, Grade 8, Science. Retrieved May 6, 2015 from http://www.cde.ca.gov/Ta/tg/sr/css05rtq.asp.

De Corte, E., Verschaffel, L., & De Win, L. (1985). Influence of rewording verbal problems on children's problem representations and solutions. *Journal of Educational Psychology*, 77(4), 460–470.

Ercikan, K. (2006). Developments in assessment of student learning and achievement. In P. A. Alexander and P. H. Winne (Eds.), American Psychological Association, Division 15, *Handbook of educational psychology*, 2nd edition (pp. 929–952). Mahwah, NJ: Lawrence Erlbaum Associates.

Ericsson, K. A. & Simon, H. S. (1993). *Protocol analysis: Verbal reports as data*. Cambridge, MA: The MIT Press.

Gay, G. (2010). *Culturally responsive teaching*, 2nd edition. New York: Teachers College Press.

Gierl, M. J., Rogers, W. T., & Klinger, D. (1999, April). Using statistical and judgmental reviews to identify and interpret translation DIF. Paper presented at the annual meeting of the National Council on Measurement in Education, Montreal, QC.

Haladyna, T. M., Downing, S. M., & Rodriguez, M. C. (2002). A review of multiple-choice item-writing guidelines for classroom assessment. *Applied Measurement in Education* 15(3), 309–334.

Hambleton, R. & Rodgers, J. (1995). Item bias review. *Practical Assessment, Research & Evaluation*, 4(6). Retrieved April 10, 2012 from http://PAREonline.net/getvn.asp?v=4&n=6.

Hambleton, R. K. & Jirka, S. J. (2006). Anchor-based methods for judgmentally estimating item statistics. In S. M. Downing & T. M. Haladyna (Eds.), *Handbook of test development* (pp. 399–420). Mahwah, NJ: Lawrence Erlbaum Associates, Publishers.

Hambleton, R. K. & Jones, R. W. (1994). Comparison of empirical and judgmental procedures for detecting differential item functioning. *Educational Research Quarterly*, 18, 21–36.

Herman, J. L. & Baker, E. L. (2005). Making benchmark testing work for accountability and improvement: Quality matters. *Educational Leadership*, 63(3), 48–55.

Hood, S. (1998). Culturally responsive performance-based assessment: Conceptual and psychometric considerations. *The Journal of Negro Education*, 67, 3, 187–196.

Kachchaf, R. R. (2011). Exploring problem solving strategies on multiple-choice science items: Comparing native Spanish-speaking English language learners and mainstream monolinguals. Unpublished doctoral dissertation. University of Colorado Boulder.

Kane, M. (2006). Content-related validity evidence in test development. In S. M. Downing & T. M. Haladyna (Eds.), *Handbook of test development* (pp. 131–153). Mahwah, NJ: Lawrence Erlbaum Associates, Publishers.

Kieffer, M. J., Lesaux, N. K., Rivera, M., & Francis, D. J. (2009). Accommodations for English language learners taking large-scale assessments: A meta-analysis on effectiveness and validity. *Review of Educational Research*, 79(3), 1168–1201.

Kopriva, R. J. (Ed.) (2008). *Improving testing for English language learners*. New York: Routledge.

Koretz, D. (2008). *Measuring up: What educational testing really tell us.* Cambridge, MA: Harvard University Press.

Kress, G. & van Leeuwen, T.(2001). *Multimodal discourse: The modes and media of contemporary communication.* Oxford, UK: Oxford University Press.

Ladson-Billings, G.(1995). Toward a theory of culturally relevant pedagogy. *American Research Journal. 32*(3) 465–491.

Leighton, J. & Gierl, M. (2007). Verbal reports as data for cognitive diagnostic assessment. In J. Leighton & M. Gierl (Eds.), *Cognitive diagnostic assessment for education: Theory and applications* (pp. 146–172). Cambridge University Press.

Lemke, J. L. (2003). Mathematics in the middle: Measure, picture, gesture, sign, and word. In M. Anderson, A. Sáenz-Ludlow, S. Zellweger, S., & V.V. Cifarelli (Eds.), *Educational perspectives on mathematics as semiosis. From thinking to interpreting to knowing* (pp. 215–234). Ottawa: Legas.

Martiniello, M. (2008). Language and the performance of English-language learners in math word problems. *Harvard Educational Review, 78*(2), 333–368.

Martiniello, M. (2009). Linguistic complexity, schematic representations, and differential item functioning for English language learners in math tests. *Educational Assessment, 14*, 160–179.

Mayer, R. E. (2005). Cognitive theory of multimedia learning. Introduction to multimedia learning. In R. E. Mayer (Ed.), *The Cambridge handbook of multimedia learning* (pp. 1–16). Cambridge, NY: Cambridge University Press.

Megone, M. E., Cai, J., Silver, E. A., & Wang, N. (1994). Validating the cognitive complexity and content quality of a mathematics performance assessment. *International Journal of Educational Research, 21*(3), 317–340.

Morgan, C. (1998). *Writing mathematically: The discourse investigation.* London: Falmer Press.

Murphy, A., Bailey, A., & Butler, F. (2006). *California English language development standards and assessment: Evaluating linkage and alignment.* Study conducted by CTB/McGraw-Hill for the State of California Department of Education.

National Assessment Governing Board, US Department of Education(2008). *Science assessment and item specifications for the 2009 National Assessment of Educational Progress.* Washington, DC: Author.

National Assessment Governing Board, US Department of Education(2010). *Content alignment studies of the 2009 National Assessment of Educational Progress for Grade 12 reading and mathematics with SAT and ACCUPLACER assessments of these subjects.* Washington, DC: Author.

Nisbett, R. E. & Miyamoto, Y. (2005). The influence of culture: holistic versus analytic perception. *TRENDS in Cognitive Sciences, 9*(10), 467–473.

Noble, T., Rosebery, A., Suarez, C., Warren, B., & O'Connor, M. C. (2014). Science assessments and English language learners: Validity evidence based on response processes. *Applied Measurement in Education, 27*(4), 248–260.

Norman, D. (2013). *The design of everyday things: Revised and expanded edition.* New York: Basic Books.

Pellegrino, J. W., Chudowsky, N., & Glaser, R. (2001). *Knowing what students know: The science and design of educational assessment.* Washington, DC: National Academy Press.

Popham, J. W. (2012). *Assessment bias: How to banish it, second edition.* Boston: Pearson Education, Inc.

Porter, A. C. (2002). Measuring the content of instruction: Uses in research and practice. *Educational Researcher, 31*(7), 3–14.

Porter, A., Smithson, J., Blank, R., & Zeidner, T. (2007). Alignment as a teacher variable. *Applied Measurement in Education, 20*, 27– 51.

Ruiz-Primo, M. A., Li, M., Wills, K., Giamellaro, M., Lan, M. -C., Mason, H., & Sands, D. (2012). Developing and evaluating instructionally sensitive assessments in science. *Journal of Research in Science Teaching, 49*(6), 691–712.

Ruiz-Primo, M. A., Shavelson, R. J., Hamilton, L., & Klein, S. (2002). On the evaluation of systemic science education reform: Searching for instructional sensitivity. *Journal of Research in Science Teaching, 39*(5), 369–393.

Ruiz-Primo, M. A., Shavelson, R. J., Li, M., & Schutlz, S. E., (2001). On the validity of cognitive interpretations of scores from alternative mapping techniques. *Educational Assessment, 7*(2), 99–141.

Saffer, D. (2014). *Microinteractions: designing with details.* Sebastopol, CA: O'Reilly.

Sato, E., Lagunoff, R., Worth, P., Bailey A. L., & Butler, F. A. (2005). *ELD standards linkage and test alignment under Title III: A pilot study of the CELDT and the California ELD and content standards.* Final report (June) to the California Department of Education, Sacramento, CA.

Schmidt, W. H., McKnight, C. C., & Raizen, S. A. (with Jakwerth, P. M., Valverde, G. A., Wolfe, R. G., Britton, E. D., Bianchi, L. J., & Houang, R. T.)(1996). *A splintered vision: An investigation of U.S. science and mathematics education.* Dordrecht, The Netherlands: Kluwer Academic Publishers.

Schnotz, W. (2005). An integrated model of text and picture comprehension. In R. E. Mayer (Ed.), *The Cambridge handbook of multimedia learning* (pp. 49–69). Cambridge, NY: Cambridge University Press.

Shaftel, J., Belton-Kocher, E., Glasnapp, D., & Poggio, G. (2006). The impact of language characteristics in mathematics test items on the performance of English language learners and students with disabilities. *Educational Assessment, 11*(2), 105–126.

Solano-Flores, G. & Kidron, Y. (2006). *Formal and judgmental approaches in the analysis of test item linguistic complexity: A comparative study.* Paper presented at the annual meeting of the American Educational Research Association, San Francisco, California, April 8–12.

Solano-Flores, G.(2006). Language, dialect, and register: Sociolinguistics and the estimation of measurement error in the testing of English-language learners. *Teachers College Record, 108*(11), 2354–2379.

Solano-Flores, G. (2011). *Assessing the cultural validity of assessment practices: An introduction.* In M. R. Basterra, E. Trumbull, & G. Solano-Flores (Eds.), *Cultural validity in assessment: Addressing linguistic and cultural diversity* (pp. 3–21). New York: Routledge.

Solano-Flores, G. & Gustafson, M. (2013). Assessment of English language learners: A critical, probabilistic, systemic view. In M. Simon, K. Ercikan, & M. Rousseau (Eds.), *Improving large scale assessment in education: Theory, issues, and practice* (pp. 87–109). New York: Taylor & Francis: Routledge.

Solano-Flores, G. & Li, M. (2009). Generalizability of cognitive interview-based measures across cultural groups. *Educational Measurement: Issues and Practice, 28*(2), 9–18.

Solano-Flores, G. & Nelson-Barber, S.(2001). On the cultural validity of science assessments. *Journal of Research in Science Teaching, 38*(5), 553–573.

Solano-Flores, G. & Trumbull, E. (2003). Examining language in context: The need for new research and practice paradigms in the testing of English-language learners. *Educational Researcher, 32*(2), 3–13.

Solano-Flores, G. & Wang, C. (2015). Complexity of illustrations in PISA–2009 science items and its relationship to the performance of students from Shanghai, China, the United States, and Mexico. *Teachers College Record, 117*(1), 1–18.

Solano-Flores, G., Lara., J., Sexton, U., & Navarrete, C. (2001). *Testing English language learners: A sampler of student responses to science and mathematics test items.* Washington, DC: Council of Chief State School Officers.

Solano-Flores, G., Wang, C., Kachchaf, R., Soltero-Gonzalez, L., & Nguyen-Le, K. (2014). Developing testing accommodations for English language learners: Illustrations as visual supports for item accessibility. *Educational Assessment, 19,* 267–283.

Vygotsky, L. S. (1978). *Mind in society: The development of higher psychological processes.* Cambridge, MA: Harvard University Press.

Wang, C. (2012). *The use of illustrations in large-scale science assessment: A comparative study.* Doctoral dissertation. University of Colorado Boulder.

Webb, N. L., Alt, M., Ely, R., & Vesperman, E. (2005). *Web alignment tool (WAT) training manual.* Madison, WI: Wisconsin Center for Educational Research.

Webb. N. L.(2007). Issues related to judging the alignment of curriculum standards and assessments. *Applied Measurement in Education, 20*(1), 7–25.

Welch, C. (2006). Item and prompt development in performance testing. In S. M. Downing & T. M. Haladyna, *Handbook of test development* (pp. 303–327). Mahwah, NJ: Lawrence Erlbaum Associates, Publishers.

Winter, P., Kopriva, R. J., Chen, S. and Emick, J.(2006). Exploring individual and item factors that affect assessment validity for diverse learners: Results from a large-scale cognitive lab. *Learning and individual differences, 16*(2006), 267–276.

Young, J. W. (2009). A framework for test validity research on content assessments taken by English language learners. *Educational Assessment, 14,* 122–138.

Zieky, M. (2006). Fairness reviews in assessment. In S. M. Downing & T. M. Haladyna (Eds.), *Handbook of test development* (pp. 359–376). Mahwah, NJ: Lawrence Erlbaum Associates, Publishers.

9

ITEM AND TEST PSYCHOMETRIC PROPERTIES

Overview

This chapter discusses test review based on the *psychometric properties* of tests and items—quantifiable attributes that can be used as indicators of the technical quality of educational measurement instruments—and the overall judgment of the quality of tests, mainly on reliability and validity. Typically, these judgments are made by educational measurement specialists (psychometricians) as part of the process of test development. While the aspects of validity concerning evidence on content and evidence on response processes were discussed in Chapter 8, this chapter discusses the relations of the scores of a test with other variables as a source of validity evidence.

Rather than providing rigorous definitions and technical explanations, the chapter is intended to support educators to understand the reasoning used by psychometricians when they construct tests and evaluate their quality in large-scale assessment contexts. Understanding these properties helps educators to make informed decisions when they select and use commercially available tests and to properly interpret reports on the performance of their ELL students on both English proficiency and content knowledge tests. Ultimately, understanding how tests are reviewed based on their psychometric properties helps educators to become critical users of tests.

The basic concepts discussed originate from the three psychometric theories: classical theory, item response theory, and generalizability theory. Because the chapter does not attempt to provide exhaustive discussions, the simplest definitions and perspectives have been chosen to discuss concepts that may be viewed and defined differently depending on the psychometric theory used.

The section "Item Properties" provides definitions of properties of items that are essential to examining the quality of tests and are especially important in the assessment of ELL students. The section also discusses score correlation and test score differences. The section "Reliability" explains different forms in which the consistency of measures can be examined depending on the characteristics of tests.

The section "Validity Evidence Based on the Relations of Test Scores" discusses how evidence on the relations of the scores of a test with other variables inform the evaluative judgment on the extent to which sound generalizations can be made about students based on the scores of a test.

Item Properties

As part of the process of test development, the psychometric properties of items need to be examined to determine which items need to revised or even discarded if these properties are below certain standards of quality. The intended outcome of this review is a pool or configuration of items that, altogether, contribute to the high quality of the instrument.

Even after trying out the items with pilot samples of students, the psychometric properties of some items may be found to not be appropriate (Ercikan, 2002; Roth, Oliveri, Sandilands, Lyons-Thomas, & Ercikan, 2013). This may be especially the case when subpopulations (e.g. ELL students, non-ELL students) are disaggregated and analyses are conducted to examine the psychometric properties of the items separately for each subpopulation. These analyses may reveal, for example, that the psychometric properties of items are within acceptable standards of quality for mainstream students but below those standards for ELL students. However, it is important to keep in mind that the presence of an item with poor psychometric properties does not necessarily imply that the entire test is flawed.

Item Difficulty

The difficulty of an item can be examined in terms of attributes such as the complexity of the knowledge it is intended to assess and the sets of cognitive demands imposed on the test taker. In the context of large-scale assessment, difficulty needs to be operationalized and quantified. An item that is easy is an item to which many students respond correctly; an item that is difficult is an item to which few students respond correctly. Thus, *item difficulty* is defined as the proportion of students who respond correctly to an item (see Livingston, 2006).

The indicator of item difficulty is commonly referred to as the p-value, a coefficient that ranges between 0 (a value that is possible when no student responds correctly to an item) and 1 (a value that is possible when all students respond correctly to the item). The p-value should not be confused with the "p" used to report levels of statistical significance of data. For dichotomous items (i.e. those items which are scored as either correct or incorrect), the p-value is computed by dividing the number of students who respond to it correctly by the total number of students who were given that item (Note 9.1). A variation of this simple formula (not discussed here) exists for partial-credit items.

A frequent misconception on item difficulty is that items of high quality are those to which are responded correctly by the majority of examinees. In actuality, an item that is too easy (too many students respond to it correctly) or too difficult (to many students fail to respond correctly to it) is useless to assessment purposes. Roughly, for multiple-choice items with four options, a p-value that is higher or lower than certain values (say, above 0.80 and below 0.60) indicates that an item needs to be revised.

Item Discrimination

Item discrimination is the ability of an item to distinguish between students who have and students who do not have the knowledge and skills assessed by an instrument. A good, discriminating item is likely to be answered correctly by those who obtain a high score on the test and to be answered incorrectly by those who obtain a low score on the test. A *discrimination index* ranges between the values of −1 and 1. An index of 0 indicates that equal proportions of the high performing and low performing students respond correctly to the item; an index of 1 means that only high performing students tend to respond to the item correctly—a rare, ideal condition. A negative discrimination index means that low performing subgroups tend to respond correctly—a rare and highly undesirable condition. Normally, a discrimination index is regarded as acceptable if its value is 0.25 or higher. Few items have very high discrimination indexes.

Differential Item Functioning

Differential item functioning has been used when there is a history of bias against a given subgroup in a population of examinees or when a test is adapted to be used with a population for which it was not originally created (see Camilli, 2013). Examples of subgroups against which items may be biased are female students, low income family students, students who are given translated tests, and ELL students.

Based on item response theory (a psychometric theory of scaling), *differential item functioning* is well known as an indicator of bias in test items. An item is said to function differentially when two samples of the populations (e.g. ELL and non-ELL students) with the same degree of proficiency in the domain of knowledge have different probabilities to respond correctly to the item (see Hambleton, 1989). In ELL testing, the two groups compared are ELL students (the focal group) and non-ELL students (the reference group). Since language proficiency is the grouping factor, the differential functioning of the item is attributed to the linguistic characteristics of the item.

Research on the differential functioning of items between linguistic groups speaks to how the properties of tests are shaped by language. Subtle variations in the wording of items may determine whether or not they function differentially (Ercikan, 2002; Roth, Oliveri, Sandilands, Lyons-Thomas, & Ercikan, 2013).

While differential item functioning is a valuable indicator that can be used with the intent to ensure valid, fair testing for ELL students, there are methodological and practical limitations that need to be considered. The methodological limitations stem from the fact that the procedures for analyzing differential item functioning are silent about heterogeneity. More specifically, the reference and focal group samples of students are assumed to be homogeneous. Yet, as discussed in Chapter 2, ELL populations are linguistically heterogeneous. Not considering this linguistic heterogeneity and treating ELL students as a single, homogeneous group may affect the ability to detect differentially functioning items. Indeed, there is evidence that the sensitivity to linguistic heterogeneity with which the samples of the students for the focal group are assembled influences the sensitivity of differential item functioning analyses (Ercikan, Roth, Simon, Sandilands, & Lyons-Thomas, 2014). The main implication of this evidence is that many differentially functioning items may go undetected if the linguistic heterogeneity of ELL populations is not properly addressed.

The practical limitations stem from the fact that, unfortunately, examining differential item functioning is costly and time consuming (Allalouf, 2003). Ideally, all the items in a test to be used with a linguistically diverse population of students should go through a process of development in which their wording is refined iteratively based on information on differential item functioning. In reality, procedures for detecting differential item functioning procedures (van der Linden & Hambleton, 1997; van der Linden & Pashley, 2010) may be difficult to use routinely with all the items in a test. The inclusion of a given item in a large-scale test is not necessarily an indication that it has gone thorough DIF scrutiny.

Information on the percentages of items that are examined for DIF or the actions that assessment systems take for items detected as differentially functioning is not usually available. The chapter "Fairness in Testing of the Standards for Educational and Psychological Testing" (AERA, APA, NCME, 2014) recognizes the need for minimizing bias in the testing of linguistically and culturally diverse groups and the need for identifying and eliminating or minimizing characteristics of items that are irrelevant to the constructs tests are intended to measure. Unfortunately, the document is not explicit enough about the minimum percentages of items used in tests that should be scrutinized for differential item functioning.

Dimensionality

Dimensionality is the term used to refer to the number of constructs assessed by a test. If a test is created with the purpose of assessing a given construct, there should be certainty that its items are unidimensional, which means that its items measure only that construct. Appropriate analyses can reveal whether an item is unidimensional or multidimensional. A multidimensional item involves different kinds of skills or knowledge in addition to the one kind of skill or knowledge that the instrument is intended to measure. Those kinds of skills or knowledge are called *latent traits*—a term that reflects the fact that they are unexpected, unobservable, or unanticipated (see Bollen, 2002). It is not difficult to see that in the assessment of ELL students, many latent traits are related to language.

Dimensionality is an important property to consider in tests and items in both content and language assessment. Dimensionality is an issue in content tests because language is the means through which tests are administered and language skills cannot be disentangled from the ability to understand the content of items and to respond to them.

Dimensionality is also an issue in language proficiency tests because many language skills are interrelated. For example, suppose that a reading comprehension test consists of questions students answer after reading literary passages. If the passages include archaic words, words of low frequency, or words with multiple meanings, the knowledge and skills involved in responding to the items involve vocabulary knowledge in addition to reading comprehension. It could be argued that individuals who are effective readers also have a good knowledge of vocabulary. However, while the two constructs are intimately related, they are not the same thing. The conclusions made about the reading comprehension of students based on their scores on the test may be erroneous due to this confounding.

Multidimensionality by itself is not necessarily a problem. The problem is to wrongly assume unidimensionality in cases in which items are multidimensional, which may lead to flawed interpretations of the results of tests. Many analyses of the properties of tests and items are based on assumptions about dimensionality. For example, the use of Cronbach's alpha, a coefficient on internal consistency of the items in a test, assumes unidimensionality. Violating the assumption of unidimensionality may lead to improper judgments about the quality of tests and items.

Score Correlation

Correlation can be thought of as the extent to which the values of two variables vary together. In the context of assessment, correlation is the extent to which students' scores on two tests, the scores given by two raters to the same students, or the scores obtained by students on the same test on different occasions vary together.

How closely and in which direction the scores vary together is described by a *correlation coefficient*, which ranges between 1 and −1. A coefficient of 1 indicates a perfect positive correlation in which the two rank orderings are identical. A coefficient of 0 indicates no relation at all between the two variables. A coefficient of −1 indicates a perfect correlation in which the two variables vary in opposite directions.

Test Score Differences

Mean score differences are the simplest indicator of achievement differences between student populations. They are used commonly to evaluate the differences between groups of students and to evaluate the effectiveness of interventions. The evaluation of the effectiveness of testing accommodations for ELL students illustrates how groups of students under different conditions are compared using test score differences.

Typically, the reports of results of score comparisons include the size of the sample of students, the mean scores obtained by students, and the standard deviation of those scores (a measure of the dispersion of the scores). Also, the reports include information on the statistical significance and the effect size of the score differences observed. The former refers to the probability that the observed differences are due to chance; the latter is the magnitude of the difference between mean scores.

Reliability

Reliability refers to the consistency of measures of academic achievement across observations in the judgment of student performance (see Haertel, 2006). Depending on the characteristics of an assessment, this consistency may be across items, across raters, across different versions of the same test, or across occasions in which students are tested. This consistency is typically evaluated in terms of a correlation.

Stability and Consistency

Reliability can take the form of *stability*. Students' scores on the same test administered several times may vary considerably, even if the tasks are exactly the same (Ruiz-Primo, Baxter, & Shavelson, 1993), which explains why decisions about examinees should not be made based on one score (see Webb, Shavelson, & Haertel, 2006).

Cronbach's alpha is a coefficient of *internal consistency reliability*. Cronbach's alpha coefficient of internal consistency is obtained with a procedure equivalent to averaging the correlations of student scores between halves for all the halves of the test that can be constructed with all the possible combinations of items (see Cronbach, 1990).

Inter-Rater Reliability

For constructed-response tests, in which the scoring of student responses involves human judgment, reliability includes *consistency between raters*. Inter-rater reliability is defined as the correlation of scores given by independent raters to the same set of student responses.

The difficulty interpreting written responses given by ELL students to constructed-response items poses a challenge to inter-rater reliability in the testing of ELLs. Due to both limited proficiency in English and influences from the native language, the responses from ELLs may be different from the responses from mainstream students due to differences in linguistic features such as sentence length, discursive style, and patterns of spelling mistakes. The importance of such differences should not be underestimated. Raters' judgments of written responses can be influenced by their degree of familiarity with discursive patterns that are not frequent in standard English. However, there is evidence that high inter-rater reliabilities can be attained in the scoring of ELL students' responses to open-ended mathematics items when the raters have the same linguistic backgrounds as those of the students whose responses they score (Solano-Flores & Li, 2009).

In the context of large-scale testing, matching raters with students according to their linguistic backgrounds poses serious logistical challenges. These challenges stem from the fact that, as with ELL students, raters vary tremendously in their proficiency in reading and different levels of familiarity with the academic language of their first language. This makes it necessary to examine inter-rater reliability when raters' backgrounds are different form those of the students whose responses they score. There is evidence that bilingual teachers who have learned the ELL students' first language as a second language and bilingual teachers whose first language is that of the ELLs produce comparable scores of ELLs tested in English for short, open-ended responses (Kachchaf & Solano-Flores, 2012). This finding suggests that individuals with different linguistic backgrounds can be trained to reliably score the responses of ELLs. Research on the assessment of writing skills indicates that, with proper training, raters whose language background is different to that of the examinees can reliably score those students' writing (Shohamy, Gordon, & Kraemer, 2010).

Sampling and Reliability

The notion of sampling allows understanding of reliability in its multiple forms. Small sizes of the samples of observations tend to produce inaccurate estimates of the knowledge or skill being measured. To minimize measurement error, the size of the sample (i.e. the number) of items, occasions, or raters needs to be increased. Based on the amount of measurement error due to these sources and their interaction, it is possible to determine the minimum number of items, occasions, or raters that should be used in a test to obtain high-quality measures of academic achievement (see Shavelson & Webb, 2009).

Validity Based on the Relations of Test Scores

A minimum degree of certainty should exist that any score differences between students are due to differences in the construct being measured, not other sources.

As discussed in Chapter 8, the notion of *validity* implies a theoretical rationale and an integrated, evaluative judgment of the empirical evidence about the degree to which appropriate generalizations about the students' knowledge and skills can be made based on test scores (Kane, 2006; Messick, 1989, 1995). An important implication of this notion is that validity does not hold regardless of context or regardless of the populations with which that test is used.

One important source of evidence on validity concerns the ways in which the scores of a test are related to scores on other tests or to other variables (AERA, APA, & NCME, 2014). Three forms of validity evidence of this type are particularly important in the assessment of ELL students: convergent and discriminant evidence, test-criterion relationships, and generalization.

Convergent and Discriminant Evidence

An important form of evidence of validity is the relation of test scores to variables that are external to the test. Two forms of validity evidence are particularly important, *convergent* and *discriminant*, which are examined in terms of the extent to which the scores on a test correlate with scores on other tests that measure similar and different constructs.

Suppose that validity is examined for a literary text reading comprehension test. The test is given to a group of students for whom scores on a scientific text reading comprehension test and a vocabulary comprehension test are also available. The construct *literary text reading comprehension* is more similar to the construct *scientific text reading comprehension* than to the construct *vocabulary comprehension*. Convergent and discriminant evidence in support of the claim that the test measures literary text reading comprehension should be observed, respectively, as a higher correlation between the scores on the two reading comprehension tests and a lower correlation between the literary reading comprehension scores and the scores on the vocabulary comprehension test.

Test-Criterion Relationships

Test-criterion relationship is a form of validity evidence based on the relationship between the scores of a test and certain outcome. The extent to which the scores of the test can predict that outcome (the criterion) becomes a piece of evidence of validity (see Cole & Moss, 1989).

An example of test-criterion relationship commonly cited is the relationship between scores on college admission tests and success in college. Success in college can be operationalized as an outcome, for example, as the grade point average obtained by students in the first year of college. A reasonably high correlation between the college admission test scores and the grade point average could be used as an argument in favor of using the test to make college admissions.

One potential source of misuse or misinterpretation of this form of evidence of validity arises from the lack of an adequate theoretical framework linking the test and the criterion. Without the proper theoretical rationale justifying why a test is being used to predict the outcome, practical reasons such as low cost can lead test users to use a test beyond the original purposes for which it was created simply because its correlation with the outcome is high. As Crocker and Algina (2008, p. 225) state it, "If a simple-to-measure, immediate criterion is selected, it may not be highly related to the ultimate criterion of interest."

It is not difficult to see that, given the complexity of language constructs and the heterogeneity of ELL populations, decisions concerning test-criterion validity evidence may pose serious challenges for interpretation. Suppose, for example, a cloze reading test administered in early grades in which students read passages in silence and circle the correct missing words from three choices shown in parentheses (Shinn & Shinn, cited by Farmer, 2013). Suppose also that a moderately high correlation is observed between the scores on that test and the scores on a test of reading comprehension, administered several years later. Should the cloze reading test be used as a predictor of complex reading comprehension skills and make decisions, for example, concerning the labeling of students as "at-risk" students, or concerning special education referral decisions? Clearly, in addition to examining test-criterion validity evidence, test users need to take into consideration the theoretical defensibility of the assumed relationship between the constructs involved, and the implications of false positive and false negative decisions.

Generalization

Generalization can be thought of as the extent to which conclusions made based on the scores on a test hold beyond that test. For example, could the results of a given test be assumed to be the same if the test were given to different student populations, if it were administered under different circumstances, or if it contained different types of tasks? The topic of generalization is particularly important in the assessment of ELL students because research on assessment does not always include ELL students, yet the findings from this research may be generalized to these students.

Most likely, evidence on generalization is the aspect of validity least frequently examined in the testing of ELL students. This is especially serious considering that a way of thinking about validity is as the extent to which appropriate generalizations can be made regarding the students' knowledge or skills based on the scores produced by a test (Cronbach, Gleser, Nanda, & Rajaratnam, 1972; Shavelson & Webb, 1991). At the core of validly testing ELL students is proper task sampling. Available evidence (Solano-Flores & Li, 2009; Solano-Flores & Li, 2013) indicates that the performance of ELL students on tests of academic achievement (administered either in English or in their first language) varies tremendously across tasks due to the fact that each task poses different sets of linguistic challenges and, at the same time, each ELL student has a unique of strengths and skills in the language in which the test is administered. To minimize the amount of measurement error due to this interaction of student, language, and task, it may be necessary in many cases to increase the sample size (the number) of items used in tests.

Closing Comments

Based on the psychometric properties of tests, educational measurement specialists make decisions about the quality of instruments. Two basic aspects of this quality of instruments are validity and reliability. Validity refers to the extent to which the content of an instrument can be considered as a representative sample of a domain of knowledge and skills and to the extent to which appropriate conclusions can be drawn about the students' knowledge and skills based on the scores produced by a test. Reliability refers to the consistency of observations of student performance. Among others, these observations involve different items in a test, different raters who score student performance, and different occasions in which students are tested.

While there are important analytical procedures intended to address fairness in the testing of diverse populations (including ELLs), these procedures are typically used towards the end of the process of test development (when there are limited opportunities for correction), are not sensitive enough to the linguistic heterogeneity of ELL students, and are costly.

From a sampling perspective, proper testing practices for ELL students can be examined in terms of the accuracy with which ELL populations are specified (e.g. ELL students who are users of different first languages, ELL students with different levels of English proficiency, ELL students with different first language backgrounds) and the extent to which samples of these populations are represented in multiple stages of the process of test development (e.g. as part of the pilot students with whom the wording of items is tried out for clarity). Clearly, the notion of sampling is critical to ensuring fair and valid assessment for ELL students in both the context of large-scale assessment and in the classroom context.

Exercises

Exercise 9.1: Reliability and Validity

1. Discuss whether a test can be reliable without being valid. Make sure you provide examples.
2. Select a test you use with your students or a commercially available test with which you are familiar. Identify the form of reliability that is relevant to this test. Discuss how you could use information on correlation to examine the reliability of the instrument.

3. Discuss any issues that need to be considered in order to make valid interpretations of the information provided by the test. Make sure to include ELL students in your discussion.

Exercise 9.2: Item Difficulty and Linguistic Complexity

1. Find on the Internet the website for The Nation's Report Card (which reports the results from the National Assessment of Educational Progress—NAEP) and find the Questions Tool. Select 15 items whose content and grade are the same as or as close as possible to the content and grade you teach.
2. Examine the information on difficulty. Reflect about the particular challenges that the items may pose to their ELL students.
   - How may the interaction of linguistic complexity and content difficulty account for the low p-values of some items?
   - What patterns in the design or the wording of the most difficult items may unfairly pose challenges not related to the content assessed to ELL students?
3. How could you test if there is any relationship between the linguistic features of the items and their level of difficulty in your sample of items?

Exercise 9.3: Testing Accommodations and Mean Score Differences

1. Mean test score differences have been used to evaluate the effectiveness of accommodations for ELL students. A design for evaluating this effectiveness is shown in Figure 9.1. Suppose that sufficiently large samples of ELL and non-ELL students are randomly assigned to one of two conditions—with and without certain accommodations. Using the cells' letters, describe the specific score differences between cells that need to be observed to examine the effectiveness of the accommodation in:
   - supporting ELLs to gain access to the content of items;
   - operating on English proficiency, not factors unrelated to language; and
   - reducing the score gap between ELL students and non-ELL students.

Testing Condition	Linguistic Group	
	ELL	Non-ELL
With Accommodation	a	b
Without Accommodation	d	c

FIGURE 9.1 Design for evaluating ELL testing accommodations.

Note

Note 9.1. The definition of item difficulty is based on classical theory. This definition assumes that all students are given the same set of items.

References

Allalouf, A. (2003). Revising translated differential functioning items as a tool for improving cross-lingual assessment. *Applied Measurement in Education, 16*(1), 55–73.

American Educational Research Association, American Psychological Association, and National Council for Measurement in Education (2014). *Standards for Educational and Psychological Testing.* Washington, DC: Author.

Bollen, K.A. (2002). Latent variables in psychology and the social sciences. *Annual Review of Psychology, 53*, 605–634.

Camilli, G. (2013). Ongoing issues in test fairness. *Educational Research and Evaluation: An International Journal on Theory and Practice, 19*(2–3), 104–120.

Cole, N. & Moss, P. (1989). Bias in test use. In R. L. Linn (Ed.), *Educational measurement, third edition* (pp. 2101–219). New York: American Council on Education.

Crocker, L. & Algina, J. (2008). *Introduction to classical and modern test theory.* Mason, OH: Cengage Learning.

Cronbach, L. J. (1990). *Essentials of psychological testing, 5th edition.* New York: Harper & Row, Publishers, Inc.

Cronbach, L. J., Gleser, G. C., Nanda, H., & Rajaratnam, N. (1972). *The dependability of behavioral measurements.* New York: Wiley.

Ercikan, K. (2002). Disentangling sources of differential item functioning in multi-language assessments. *International Journal of Testing, 2*, 199–215.

Ercikan, K., Roth, W. -M. Simon, M., Sandilands, D., & Lyons-Thomas, J. (2014). Inconsistencies in DIF detection for sub-groups in heterogeneous language groups. *Applied Measurement in Education, 27*, 275–285.

Farmer, E. (2013). *Examining predictive validity and rates of growth in curriculum-based measurement with English language learners in the intermediate grades.* Doctoral dissertation. Loyola University Chicago.

Haertel, E. H. (2006). Reliability. In R. L. Brennan (Ed.), *Educational measurement* (4th ed.) (pp. 65–110). Westport, CT: American Council on Education and Praeger Publishers.

Hambleton, R. K. (1989). Principles and selected applications of item response theory. In R. L. Linn (Ed.), *Educational Measurement, 3rd Edition* (pp. 147–200). New York: American Council on Education/Macmillan Publishing Company.

Kachchaf, R. & Solano-Flores, G. (2012). Rater language background as a source of measurement error in the testing of English language learners. *Applied Measurement in Education, 25*, 167–172.

Kane, M. T. (2006). Validation. In R. L. Brennan (Ed.), *Educational measurement* (4th ed.) (pp. 17–64). Westport, CT: American Council on Education and Praeger Publishers.

Livingston, S. A. (2006). Item analysis. In S. M. Downing & T. M. Haladyna (Eds.), *Handbook of test development* (pp. 421–441). Mahwah, NJ: Lawrence Erlbaum Associates, Publishers.

Messick, S. (1989). Validity. In R. L. Linn (Ed.), *Educational measurement* (3rd ed.) (pp. 13–103). Washington, DC: American Council on Education and National Council on Measurement in Education.

Messick, S. (1995). Validity of psychological assessment: Validation of inferences from persons' responses and performance as scientific inquiry into score meaning. *American Psychologist, 50*(9), 741–749.

Roth, W. -M., Oliveri, M. E., Sandilands, D., Lyons-Thomas, J., & Ercikan, K. (2013). Investigating sources of differential item functioning using expert think-aloud protocols. *International Journal of Science Education, 35*, 546–576.

Ruiz-Primo, M. A., Baxter, G. P., & Shavelson, R. J.(1993). On the stability of performance assessments. *Journal of Educational Measurement, 30*(1), 41–53.

Shavelson, R. J. & Webb, N. M.(1991). *Generalizability theory: A primer.* Newbury Park, CA: Sage.

Shavelson, R. J. & Webb, N. M.(2009). Generalizability theory and its contribution to the discussion of the generalizability of research findings. In K. Ercikan & W. -M. Roth (Eds.), *Generalizing from educational research: Beyond qualitative and quantitative polarization* (pp. 13–31). New York: Routledge.

Shohamy, E., Gordon, C. M., & Kraemer, R. (2010). The effect of raters' background and training on the reliability of direct writing tests. *The Modern Language Journal, 76*(1), 27–33.

Solano-Flores, G. & Li, M. (2009). Language variation and score variation in the testing of English language learners, native Spanish speakers. *Educational Assessment, 14*, 1–15.

Solano-Flores, G. & Li, M. (2013). Generalizability theory and the fair and valid assessment of linguistic minorities. *Educational Research and Evaluation, 19*(2–3), 245–263.

van der Linden, W. J. & Hambleton, R. K. (Eds.)(1997). *Handbook of modern item response theory.* New York: Springer.

van der Linden, W. J. & Pashley, P. J.(2010). Item selection and ability estimation in adaptive testing. In W. J. Van der Linden & C. A. W. Glas (Eds.), *Elements of adaptive testing* (pp. 3–30). Monterey, CA: CTB/McGraw-Hill

Webb, N. M., Shavelson, R. J., & Haertel, E. H.(2007). Reliability coefficients and generalizability theory. In C. R. Rao & S. Sinharay (Eds.), *Handbook of statistics: Psychometrics* (Vol. 26, pp. 81–124). Amsterdam: Elsevier B. V.

INDEX